Chapter 1 – Introduction

I0492573

Superannuation is like a savings account used to put money aside for taxpayers (individual people) until they reach retirement or preservation age. The superannuation money is usually paid by an employer towards a nominated superannuation fund of the employee, and this amount is set at 9.5% of the total gross earnings of the employee. The ever-growing Self-Managed Superannuation Fund (SMSF) industry in Australia is a way for individuals to have more control over their retirement money in terms of investing in different assets, or different classes of assets, which other industry superannuation funds are less likely to invest in, or have a direct investment in.

There are two different authorities that govern superannuation in Australia. The body that oversees the large industry superannuation funds, such as HESTA, Host Plus, CBUS, is the Australian Prudential Regulation Authority (APRA). The body that governs, or oversees the SMSFs is the Australian Taxation Office (ATO).

The COVID-19 pandemic has led to some changes in superannuation, and these changes will not be discussed at length in this book, because the ATO website has information that is up to date.

So what is an SMSF? Dixon Advisory defines an SMSF as "a superannuation trust structure that provides benefits to its members upon retirement. The main difference between SMSFs and other super funds is that SMSF members are also the trustees of the fund. SMSFs can have between one and four members, and one of the main advantages is the level of control that trustees have when it comes to tailoring the fund to meet their individual needs".

Why do more and more people choose to set up and operate a SMSF? One of the reasons is that they like to be in control of where their investment money is going, and be able to have a direct investment in particular types of assets. Another reason may be that a person is running a business, and wants to have the SMSF own that business property, so that the person can pay rent to the SMSF and at the same time benefit from the income, especially if the person is at retirement or preservation age.

There are advantages and disadvantages in setting up and maintaining a SMSF, and in order to consider whether this is for you, the advantages must be greater than the disadvantages. There are also taxation concessions and implications in having a SMSF. The tax concessions are that the SMSF is taxed at 15% of its taxable income (assessable income minus deductions), and taxed at 1/3 (or 10%) of any capital gains that the SMSF derives. However, there are tax implications if a breach of the superannuation rules occurs, possible fines and penalties, non-compliance status and the SMSF will be taxed at 45% of its income and assets. That is very hefty. However, your accountant or tax agent will guide you to ensure you do not breach, or continue to breach, the superannuation provisions in your SMSF.

Some advantages of having a SMSF are:

- you can have up to four members and the funds stay directly in your SMSF for the benefit of the members until they reach retirement age.
- You have total control over the SMSF in relation to investing in different assets and different types of assets.
- You can invest in assets that a large superannuation fund will less likely invest in. E.g. if you are running a business, your SMSF can own the property and therefore generate good rental returns in the SMSF.
- The SMSF trust deed allows you to borrow in order to grow your SMSF portfolio (this will be discussed later).
- The tax rate is 15% of the SMSF taxable income (assessable income minus deductions).
- The capital gains tax rate is 10% in the SMSF.
- Tax losses can be carried forward.
- If the SMSF is in pension phase (this will be discussed later), there is no tax liability, except for the ATO Supervisory Levy ($259.00 currently). All income will be exempt pension income.

- If the fund is in pension phase, the pension payments to members are tax-free in the hands of the member. Any income or capital gain derived in the SMSF is effectively tax-free.

Some disadvantages of having a SMSF are:

- If you have a small amount of funds, this will be taken due to the costs of operating and maintaining the fund, i.e. accounting fees, auditor's remuneration.
- The funds in your SMSF are not available for you until you reach retirement (usually after 60 years old) or preservation age (generally between 55 and 59).
- SMSFs are restricted in how the funds are used. E.g. you cannot have the SMSF 'lend money' to its members. This is providing financial assistance to members before reaching preservation age, and this is against the Superannuation Industry (Supervision) Regulations Act 1984 (SIS Act).

The taxation concessions and implications will be discussed in more detail over the coming chapters. The first thing that you should always ask yourself before setting up a SMSF is, why do I want to set up a SMSF? What benefit will I receive from this, as compared to what I am already receiving from my existing super? If you already have answers to these questions, then you will be in a good position to decide whether you want, or need, to set up a SMSF, or whether it is not the right option for you at this stage. It may be a good option in the future, but may not be beneficial to you right now, depending on your circumstances.

This short book will not bore you with statistics and numbers, but seeks to present clear explanations on what can be done, and what cannot be done, in a SMSF.

References:

Australian Taxation Office (ATO)   -
https://www.ato.gov.au/Super/Self-managed-super-funds/

Dixon Advisory - https://www.dixon.com.au/smsf/what-is-an

Chapter 2 - Setting up your SMSF

Now that you have thought about starting a SMSF and evaluated whether this is the way for you to go, this section will guide you through the steps involved in setting up your SMSF. Usually, your accountant or tax agent will do this for you, and the one-off set up cost will likely be in the range of $1,000 to $2,000 depending on the accountant and the online service that your accountant uses. The advantage of this is that it saves you time and effort in doing it by yourself.

You need to be aware before delving into setting up your SMSF, there is a sole purpose test that is required to be maintained throughout the life of the SMSF. According to the ATO, "your SMSF needs to meet the sole purpose test to be eligible for the tax concessions normally available to super funds. This means your fund needs to be maintained for the sole purpose of providing retirement benefits to your members, or to their dependants if a member dies before retirement.

Contravening the sole purpose test is very serious. In addition to the fund losing its concessional tax treatment, trustees could face civil and criminal penalties.

For example, it's likely your fund will not meet the sole purpose test if you or anyone else, directly or indirectly, obtains a financial benefit when making investment decisions and arrangements (other than increasing the return to your fund).

When investing in collectables such as art or wine, you need to make sure that SMSF members don't have use of, or access to, the assets of the SMSF.

Your fund fails the sole purpose test if it provides a pre-retirement benefit to someone – for example, personal use of a fund asset."

Having now considered the sole purpose test, if you do not have a large amount to set up a SMSF, then maybe now is not the right time, due to the cost of setting up the fund and the annual costs of operating the fund. However, it is assumed that you have a decent amount to be able to set up, operate and maintain your SMSF.

If you wish to set up your SMSF by yourself, you will save the one-off cost but you need to take time and extra care to ensure all the information you provide online is correct and up to date. One website that is recommended is www.trustdeed.com.au. This website enables you to set up your SMSF, and after inputting all your relevant information, you will be provided with a SMSF Trust Deed along with the rest of the documents to prove that the SMSF is registered.

The following steps need to be considered when setting up your SMSF:

1. What is the name of your SMSF? For demonstration purposes, we will use ABC Superannuation Fund.
2. Who will be the trustee/s? You will have come across the term trustee and Trust before. Basically, a SMSF is a Trust, but unlike a normal Trust, the funds in your SMSF is not available to you until you reach retirement or preservation age. We will discuss a company trustee and individual trustee later in this chapter. For this purpose, let us choose the trustee company as ABC Pty Ltd. For a company trustee, there will be a fee payable to the Australian Securities & Investment Commission (ASIC) upon registering the company, and the annual ASIC fee will be around $55.00, as this company will only serve as a trustee for the SMSF. It is a

special purpose company, so the registration fee will not be around $270 each year like a normal company.

3. Who will be the member/s of the SMSF? You can have from one to four members according to the SIS Regulations.
4. Who will be the director/s of the trustee company? Please note that if you are setting up a trustee company, then each member of the SMSF must also be directors of the trustee company.
5. Who will be the shareholder/s of the trustee company?
6. Enter all your information, including addresses and dates of birth as required when registering your SMSF and trustee company.
7. You must apply for an Australian Business Number (ABN) and Tax File Number (TFN) for the SMSF. This is available when completing the registration process. However, you do not apply for an ABN and TFN for the Trustee Company because it cannot trade in its own capacity. It is solely acting as a trustee for your SMSF.

After putting all this information in the online system, the website (for demonstration purpose we will use www.trustdeed.com.au) sends all this to ASIC and to their solicitors to prepare the SMSF Trust Deed and Company Constitution. In a matter of minutes, you will receive an email with all the documents to verify that the SMSF and Trustee Company are both registered and set up. You will also receive the ABN notice for your SMSF by email. A TFN notice will also be mailed you your address that you included while setting up your SMSF.

Having set up your SMSF and received all the documents, the Trust Deed is not required to be stamped, and stamping amount is not required to be paid for an SMSF Trust Deed. The Trust Deed is a legal document that is prepared for the trustee/s of the SMSF that enable the SMSF to invest in any type of asset, and also enable it to borrow for a specific asset. The Trust Deed covers the areas of the SIS regulations and is recommended to be updated every 3-4 years to incorporate changes in the superannuation and SMSF laws. One recommendation with the Trust Deed is for you to get the front page and the execution section certified by a qualified person, usually your accountant, lawyer or financial adviser.

You need to keep all the records of the Trust Deed, ABN, TFN and Trustee Company documents somewhere on your computer and have a back-up, as these are very important documents.

The next step is that you need to open a bank account for your SMSF. The bank can be a bank of your preference, and the name of the account will need to be, for example, ABC Pty Ltd ATF, or, ITF ABC Superannuation Fund. You will need to quote your SMSF ABN and possibly the Australian Company Number (ACN) of the Trustee Company, along with its name.

Later on, you can also create a share trading account in the name of your SMSF, preferably with the same bank that your SMSF account is in. Otherwise, you can use a broker if you have a good relationship with one, but usually the brokerage fees will be a little higher and there will be advisory and administration costs.

Previously in this section, you read about a corporate, or company trustee and an individual trustee/s. What is the difference, and what are the pros and cons of having either as trustee for your SMSF?

If you are the only member of your SMSF (there is no law against that), you must have a company trustee, and cannot be an individual trustee. If you wish to set up your SMSF as an individual trustee, then you must have someone else to act as another trustee in your SMSF. That person does not need to be a member.

If you have a spouse and you both wish to be members, then you have two options in your SMSF - you can both be individual trustees and members of your SMSF, or you can have a company trustee, but both members must be directors of the company trustee, and cannot be disqualified persons listed on the ASIC register.

If you have children and wish for them to be members of your SMSF, you can have up to two children, because an SMSF can have up to four members, so you, your spouse and two children, or perhaps if you have only one son/daughter, then they can be a third member. Please bear in mind that if you have a company trustee, then all SMSF members, children included, must be directors of the company trustee. What if a son/daughter is a minor (under 18 years)? The company law allows a minor director, but he/she will not be able to serve in their functions as directors until they reach 18 years old. In this case, the adult member/s of the SMSF will have the power of attorney to sign on behalf of their son/daughter who is a minor. In the case of a SMSF trustee company, this will not be complicated, because the company is there to act solely as a trustee for the SMSF.

So now that you have decided the SMSF structure, the advantages of a company trustee are:

- Companies have the benefit of limited liability. Therefore, if a company trustee suffers any liability, the individual directors will not suffer personal liability (other than in exceptional circumstances). On the other hand, an individual who acts as trustee exposes their personal assets if they incur any liability as trustee of an SMSF or other trust: if the individual's right of indemnity against the SMSF is not sufficient to discharge the liability, then the individual is still liable for the shortfall.
- A company continues to function even after the death of one of its directors, therefore, the control of a SMSF or other trust can continue even after the death of an individual SMSF member/director.
- It is easier for a corporate trustee to ensure that trust assets are kept separate from the personal assets of SMSF members.
- It can be simple and more cost effective to make changes to the directors and members.
- Legal ownership of the SMSF assets does not change when a member or director is removed.

On the other hand, SMSF company trustees also have some disadvantages, including:

- additional expenses – because you're setting up a company, there are more establishment and running costs involved (unless you set up a special purpose company whose only purpose is to act as your SMSF trustee; in this case, the running costs can be reduced, and you don't have to lodge an additional tax return for the company, only for your SMSF).
- your SMSF is also bound by corporation legislation and the trustee company must comply with ASIC and the Corporations Act 2001.

Some advantages of having an individual trustee/s are:

- no ASIC forms to complete to establish the SMSF;
- no ongoing ASIC reporting obligations to comply with; and
- fewer procedural issues to deal with, as there are more flexible requirements for holding trustee meetings and no need to comply with a company constitution.

However, the disadvantages of having an individual trustee/s are:

- always having to have two trustees, which can cause some issues especially when an individual trustee dies or becomes mentally unfit to continue acting as a trustee, or becomes disqualified.
- it may be time consuming and tedious to add or remove members and change the ownership of your assets.
- having trustees as legal owner of assets can easily lead to SMSF and personal assets inadvertently being mixed, for example, the name of the assets are in individual names, and must contain the following 'ATF'. If this is not the case, then there can be errors when preparing and lodging annual tax returns.
- Declarations of trust may be required for certain asset types, such as property.
- ATO administrative penalties apply to each individual trustee. This can result in penalties of up to four times that of a corporate trustee.

Now that you have weighed the pros and cons of using a trustee company versus individual trustees, you are in a good position to decide on whether to set up a company trustee, or have at least two individuals act as trustees in your SMSF.

References:

Australian Taxation Office -

https://www.ato.gov.au/super/self-managed-super-funds/investing/sole-purpose-test/#:~:text=Your%20SMSF%20needs%20to%20meet,a%20member%20dies%20before%20retirement.

Dixon Advisory - https://www.dixon.com.au/smsf/smsf-trustee-individual-or-corporate

Thomson Reuters Cleardocs -

https://www.cleardocs.com/clearlaw/superannuation/smsf-corporate-individual-differences.html

Chapter 3 - Adding Funds to your SMSF

Having set up your SMSF and established it, you are now ready to add money into your SMSF as a starting point to enable it to grow over time and provide the maximum benefits to the members. There are a number of ways that you can add funds into your SMSF. Your SMSF must first have a bank account to be able to add or bring funds into the SMSF.

Let us suppose that you have a spouse and that both of you are members in your SMSF. This means there are two members in your SMSF. Suppose that you are both employed in a particular role, and your employer pays the Superannuation Guarantee (SG) on top of your gross earnings. Let us also suppose that you both have about $30,000 each in your large superannuation fund as a result of employer contributions and fund earnings over many, many years. This means that there is a combined balance of $60,000 in your super. You will need to access a form from your super fund, called a rollover of benefits, where you will need to fill in your personal details and state how much you wish to rollover from your super fund.

You also need to provide your SMSF details in the form. Usually, these details are the ABN, TFN and the name of your SMSF. The super fund that will provide the rollover benefits will then check to see if your SMSF is a complying fund. Usually in the first year before any tax returns are prepared, there will be no information on the complying status of your SMSF. A complying status simply means that your SMSF complies with the SIS rules and the ATO regulations, and qualified for the 15% concessional tax on earnings and contributions.

Having filled the rollover form (it can be done online these days) and signed the relevant sections and sent it to your super fund, the super fund will then process the form and after a certain amount of time, when it is satisfied that your SMSF exists, will issue you with a check representing your rollover benefits. You then need to deposit the check to your SMSF bank account and it will generally appear in your account within 3 working days. When you receive the rollover benefits statement, you will see some components of your super balance. The components are tax-free and taxable, and this will be discussed in a later chapter.

So then, as a starting point, you will have a combined total of $60,000 in your SMSF, and there is no tax on this, because tax has already been paid on this balance from your super fund over the past years. The more members you have in your SMSF, the higher the balance will likely be before you even start making contributions.

Another way of adding funds into your SMSF is by way of concessional contributions. This means that you can contribute up to a maximum of $25,000 per person, per year, into your SMSF. If you are both business owners, you can claim these contributions as a tax deduction in your business tax returns, so that means $50,000 can be claimed as a tax deduction if you are both business owners in the same business. Then your SMSF will pay 15% tax on the $50,000, which is $7,500. Let us suppose your business is a company, the company will save 27.5% tax on the $50,000 contributed, which means the tax saving will be $13,750, and in turn your SMSF will pay $7,500 in contributions tax. You can already see the difference. If your business is not a company, then your tax saving will be based on your marginal rate of tax for an individual. If you are employees, your employer will contribute the 9.5% compulsory SG, which means that you will be entitled to claim a tax deduction of the difference between $25,000 and what your employer has contributed during the financial year.

From 1 July 2017, the ATO introduced the fact that an employee can make extra concessional contributions over and above the employer's 9.5% SG, as long as this is up to $25,000. The employee is able to claim this as a tax deduction. Previously, this kind of tax deduction was only available to sole-traders (self-employed) who have their own business, but it is now extended to employees.

Let us suppose that you both contributed $25,000 each by the end of the financial year, this means a combined total of $50,000, plus the already $60,000 that you have from the rollover benefits from your previous super fund. The total SMSF balance is now $110,000, and can be evenly split between you and your spouse. Please note if your spouse has more, or less in their super than you, then the balance for the two of you needs to be apportioned. For example, if your spouse had $20,000 and you had $40,000 in super prior to rolling over the benefits (combined balance $60,000), then you both contributed the maximum $25,000 each, then you will have a closing balance of $65,000 and your spouse will have a closing balance of $45,000 in your SMSF. This means that your portion of the total SMSF balance is 59% and your spouse portion is 41%.

There are provisions in the SIS and ATO regulations that allow you to contribute more than $25,000 per year, that is if in previous years you have unused concessional contributions that you can use to catch up. However, please see your professional accountant or financial adviser if you qualify for this provision.

A third way of adding funds into your SMSF, after the rollover benefits and concessional contributions have been exhausted, is that you can make what we call a non-concessional contribution. This type of contribution represents any after-tax amounts that you can contribute to, and this is not tax deductible, and in turn your SMSF will not pay tax on this, as long as the contribution falls within the maximum cap.

The maximum cap for a non-concessional contribution is $100,000 per person per year, or up to $300,000 for a period of three years. This means that if you contribute $300,000 this year, you will not be able to make non-concessional contributions until year 4. Let us suppose you both contribute $300,000 now as a non-concessional contribution. This means that your SMSF now has a total of $600,000 non-concessional contributions. Please bear in mind, if you exceed the cap limit, there will be 15% tax payable on the excess of the contributions. Not everyone can make this type of contribution freely. If you are 65-74 years old, you need to meet certain work tests to continue making non-concessional contributions. If you are above 75 years, then none of this contribution is available, except for a downsizer contribution (you can obtain information on this from the ATO website).

One other type of contribution is called an In-specie (asset) contribution. According to the ATO, this is in the form of transferring assets from a member to the SMSF. However, not all assets can qualify for this. In fact, the only assets that qualify for this type of contribution is listed shares and business real property. These must be transferred at market value, and the member making this transfer will need to declare a capital gains event in their individual tax return. Business real property generally means land or building used wholly and exclusively in a business. So, if you are a business owner and you own the premises in which your business operates, you can legally transfer the property into your SMSF. However, please see your professional accountant for more guidance. The information available online, on the ATO website, and in this book is not a substitute for financial advice.

Another contribution type which is not taxable in the SMSF is the government co-contribution, where the ATO provides up to $500 as a co-contribution into your SMSF. This occurs after you lodge your SMSF Annual Return and also your individual tax return for the same financial year. The co-contribution is available provided your individual income is within a certain range, called the income threshold, and the ATO provides guidance on what is included in the income threshold test. Information on this is available on the ATO website.

Having set out the types of contributions, let us suppose that you both now have a total super balance of $710,000 ($60,000 from rollover, $50,000 from concessional contributions and $600,000 from non-concessional contributions). Assuming no other activity has occurred up to the end of the financial year, your SMSF will be taxed on 15% of $50,000, which is $7,500, plus the SMSF will need to pay the ATO Supervisory Levy of $518.00. This is because it is the first year in which the SMSF has to lodge a tax return, so the ATO Supervisory Levy is $259.00 multiplied by 2. The total tax payable for the SMSF will be $8,018.00.

After lodging the tax return with the ATO for the first time, provided that all the information is correct and there is no material error, then the ATO will issue your SMSF with a complying status, meaning that your SMSF complies with the ATO and qualifies for the taxation concessions, and later on, qualifies for receiving government co-contributions, and paying its members tax-free pensions.

Chapter 4 - The SMSF Investment Strategy

This section will discuss something vital that must be incorporated within your SMSF. This is an investment strategy. What is that? It is a document that is prepared for the members of your SMSF that outlines the objective of the fund, where your fund will invest its money, i.e. asset allocations, considerations of risk factors in deciding the investment structure, and more. There is no set template to use, and this does not need to be sent to the ATO, but is to be kept and updated each year. Your SMSF auditor will also likely ask to see your investment strategy and may make recommendations in accordance with the SMSF's investments.

A number of issues in this chapter is taken from the SuperGuide website, which is a very useful tool to help you in creating an investment strategy. According to SuperGuide, SMSFs are required under the *Superannuation Industry (Supervision) Act 1993* "to formulate, review regularly and give effect to an investment strategy." The ATO also released further information in February 2020 around what it wants to see in an investment strategy, including that it expects more detail around investment allocation targets.

The current pandemic and subsequent market volatility created a high level of uncertainty for all investors, especially those that rely on their investment choices for their retirement incomes like SMSFs. The start of this new financial year, in particular, is therefore a very good time to reconsider investment goals and whether or not current investment strategies will facilitate them. This could mean a slight reallocation to more defensive investments, if trustees do not have long before retirement.

So, what are the components of an investment strategy? Is there a certain order to prepare one? There is no prescribed order in preparing an investment strategy, but the document must contain the following items:

- The overall objective of the fund. What does the fund seek to achieve for its members? This could be expressed in terms of generating high returns for members and having sufficient cash flow to pay any obligations that may arise, i.e. pensions to its members if the fund is in pension phase.
- Risk factors in investing in certain assets and the likely returns that each asset type is expected to provide.
- Risk considerations in relation to borrowing. Will the fund be able to service the loan?
- The overall composition of the fund's investments and their diversification. It is vital to diversify because if one asset class is not performing well, the other will likely perform well, and the unrealised losses will be minimised that way. It is advised to allocate a percentage range for each asset, e.g. listed shares expected to be 30-60% of the fund's balance;

fixed interest investment expected to be 20-40% of the fund's balance.

- Liquidity of investing in particular assets or asset classes in respect of the cash flow requirements of the fund's members.
- The ability of the fund to pay its existing and prospective liabilities, i.e. current tax liability, pensions to its members (if the SMSF is in pension phase - this will be discussed later).
- Consideration of insurance premiums, e.g. life insurance, whether the fund will or will not take up life insurance. It may be that each member has life insurance outside of the fund, and therefore the fund is not required to have a life insurance policy. At any rate, this must be included in the investment strategy.

In February 2020, the ATO stressed out that the investment strategy should be tailored and specific to the relevant situation and circumstances of the fund, and not just a document that states super legislation. It should be updated regularly to fit within the investment allocation of the fund.

There is no right or wrong in creating an investment strategy. Basically, you are thinking of what to invest in and how to allocate this, then you form it into words, and it becomes a document that should be followed.

If your SMSF is in accumulation phase, i.e. you and your spouse are below 55 years, then the investment strategy target may be for the fund to target a return of, say, 3-4% above the CPI (Consumer Price Index) each year. To do this, the fund will need to invest most of its assets in Equities, e.g. Australian, Global Listed Shares, and Property. Then you need to determine the percentage of these assets in relation to the total fund's balance.

However, if you have one asset, e.g. business real property, you need to work out how this property will generate cash for your SMSF, and this needs to be included in the investment strategy. Let us say that you have business real property, and this will take up about 80% of the fund's balance. Your strategy needs to include the fact that the property will generate cash by way of monthly rent from your business at market value, and your business (the tenant) itself will pay all of the outgoings and expenses relating to the property, thereby providing the maximum possible return for the fund and its members.

On the other hand, a single asset SMSF with a business property would not be the desired investment strategy of a SMSF paying pensions to its member/s. Pensions are not the only cash flow issue that SMSF trustees need to give consideration to. There will also be day-to-day expenses of the fund (such as auditor fees), tax requirements and potentially insurance premiums to pay for the fund's trustees.

An investment strategy of a trustee about to retire, for example, might detail how that fund was considering selling down some illiquid assets and investing them in something more liquid, such as shares, in order to prepare for ongoing pension payment requirements. Bear in mind that the minimum amounts must be paid as a pension for the fund to be complying.

There may be more complex issues where there are four members in your SMSF, say for example, you, your spouse and your sons/daughters. You and your spouse may have a different approach than your sons and/or daughters, and therefore the investment strategy needs to incorporate this but you need to keep it simple.

How do we create an investment strategy? You can use Word to create, prepare and regularly update your SMSF investment strategy. There is no prescribed template, you only need to consider the above points and tailor these points for your requirements, situation, and current circumstances. Please remember, you need to regularly monitor and review this document, e.g. once or twice per year, and make changes where necessary.

References:

Chapter 5 - Different phases in your SMSF

The SMSF has different phases, or stages that it goes through, from beginning to end. There are three main phases in a member's superannuation account, and this is incorporated into your SMSF. The phases are:

- **Accumulation Phase.** This is where a member's age is generally less than 55 years and the member is employed, self-employed, or owns a business and makes different types of contributions, as discussed in the previous chapter, into the SMSF. All earnings in this phase is taxed at 15% (this means income minus deductions) and any capital gain is taxed at 10% (1/3). There is no limit as to how much you can have in your member balance when the SMSF is in accumulation phase. For example, if your SMSF has taxable earnings of $35,000, then 15% of this is the tax liability, which is $5,250 plus $259 ATO Supervisory Levy. If your SMSF has a discounted capital gain of $10,000 included in the $35,000, the tax on the capital gain is 10%, which is $1,000, plus the normal 15% tax on the remaining $25,000, which is $3,750. The total tax will be $4,750 plus $259 ATO Supervisory Levy. You can already see the difference if a capital gains component is included in the taxable earnings of your SMSF.

In an accumulation phase, the funds in the SMSF are generally not accessible until you reach retirement, or preservation age. Only in exceptional circumstances, such as terminal medical illness, departing Australia permanently, for example, will you be allowed to access your funds. In the event of terminal illness, a certificate from two registered medical practitioners, with at least one of these a specialist in the area of your particular injury, must be supplied and accepted by the ATO before withdrawing funds. The payment will be tax-free if withdrawn within 24 months of certification.

There are other circumstances, or compassionate grounds in which you can withdraw super in accumulation phase. This is available on the ATO website. However, please note that as you withdraw super on compassionate grounds, there will be tax to pay. The tax is determined by taking into account what portion of your super balance is tax-free, and what portion is taxable.

Let us look at the different components of your super balance. These are tax-free and taxable components that are automatically calculated depending on the different types of contributions made to your SMSF.

The tax-free component is usually made up of contributions for which the SMSF does not pay tax, e.g. non-concessional contributions. No deductions have been claimed, and the fund pays no tax on this, so any part of your balance made up of non-concessional contributions is tax-free.

The taxable component comes in two sub-sections: taxed and untaxed element. The taxed element is made up of any concessional contributions where deductions have been claimed, and in which the fund has paid 15% tax. This includes the employer SG contributions, salary-sacrifice contributions, and additional concessional contributions.

The untaxed element is not very common these days. This is made up of funds that are generally run by the Commonwealth, State or Territory government departments, and are generally either public sector super schemes or constitutionally protected funds. Your super fund will outline the components in your member statement and you will see the tax-free and taxable components.

Let us give an example on how withdrawal tax works in an accumulation phase. If 30% of your portion is tax-free and 70% is taxable, and you withdraw a lump sum of $40,000, then your tax-free component will be 30% of $40,000, which is $12,000. The remaining amount, which is $28,000, will be taxed at your marginal rate plus 2% Medicare Levy, or a rate of 22%, whichever is lower. So if your marginal rate plus Medicare Levy is lower than 22%, then the tax applied will be your marginal rate plus Medicare Levy. If 22% is lower, then the tax rate applied will be 22%.

Let us say that you are taking the $40,000 as an income stream. This is basically receiving monthly income from your SMSF due to temporary incapacity. Let us use the same components, $12,000 tax-free and $28,000 taxable. In an income stream payment, the tax will be your marginal rate of tax plus 2% Medicare Levy. So, if your marginal rate of tax is 19%, then the tax on the super income stream will be 21% (including Medicare Levy) of $28,000, which is $5,880.

- **Transition to retirement Phase** is the next phase in an SMSF. This applies to a member who is generally between 55 and 59 years old, and has reached preservation age. The ATO website has a table of preservation age based on date of birth.

Date of birth	Preservation age
Before 1 July 1960	55
1 July 1960 – 30 June 1961	56
1 July 1961 – 30 June 1962	57
1 July 1962 – 30 June 1963	58
1 July 1963 – 30 June 1964	59
From 1 July 1964	60

Preservation age is not the same as pension age. If your date of birth, for example, is 3 October 1959, then your preservation age is 55, and you can enter into a transition to retirement phase, where you can take out super either in the form of a lump sum, or an income stream. If your date of birth is 23 July 1964, then your preservation age is 60, and you do not need to commence a transition to retirement phase. As you are 60 years old, generally any super that you withdraw from your SMSF is tax-free.

Let us say that your date of birth is before 1 July 1964 and you commence a transition to retirement phase. What is the minimum that you need to withdraw? The ATO states the minimum withdrawal percentage rules apply whether you are in transition to retirement, or pension phase. The withdrawal percentage if you are under 65 and in the transition to retirement phase is between 4% and 10% of your total super balance. You will first need to demonstrate that your work hours have reduced as you transition into retirement. The COVID-19 pandemic has led to the ATO to reduce the minimum withdrawal percentage by 50%, so now the minimum withdrawal percentage if you are under 65 years is 2%, and the maximum is still 10% if you are in the transition to retirement phase. The temporary minimum draw-down percentage is in effect until the 2020-21 financial year, i.e. until the year ended 30 June 2021.

How does tax work, or how much tax is payable if you commence a transition to retirement and withdraw money from your super? That depends on how you take the money. There are different ways in which you can take the money out - one way is a lump sum, and the other way is through an income stream.

Let us say, for example, that you have $1 million super balance and you commenced a transition to retirement phase. You can withdraw from 2% of the balance, which is $20,000, taking into account the COVID-19 reduced minimum draw-down rates. The maximum you can withdraw is still 10%, which will be $100,000 for a super balance of $1 million. If you take anywhere between the minimum and maximum amount as a LUMP SUM, i.e. in one payment, then this is tax-free. There is a provision in the super laws that if you withdraw a lump sum up to the low rate cap, then the amount is all tax-free. The low rate cap is $210,000 in 2019-20 financial year, and will be $215,000 in the 2020-21 financial year. Each year this increases by $5,000.

If you take $250,000 lump sum for the year ended 30 June 2020, then the first $210,000 is tax-free, and you will be taxed on $40,000 at 17% marginal tax rate, which includes the Medicare Levy. So effectively, the tax you pay on the $40,000 will be $6,800.

Therefore, in order to save tax, you may take up to $210,000 in one go, and this will be tax-free.

What if you want to take an income stream? This represents monthly payments from your SMSF to your personal account. Suppose you take $40,000 as an income stream in addition to your existing employment income. This $40,000 may be all taxable, depending on the components that make up the $40,000. If it is all taxable, then the tax on this income stream of $40,000 will be your marginal tax minus a 15% superannuation tax offset. So if your marginal tax rate is 32.5% plus Medicare Levy 2%, this is 34.5%, but minus 15% offset, effectively the tax on the $40,000 income stream will be $7,800 (19.5% of $40,000). 19.5% is after subtracting the 15% offset from your marginal rate of 34.5%.

You can see the tax saving if you take the $40,000 as a lump sum, as compared to taking it as an income stream. If you take it as a lump sum, the whole amount is tax-free, as it falls below the low rate cap. If you take it as an income stream, the tax you will pay on $40,000 is $7,800.

Please bear in mind that a transition to retirement phase is not a pension phase, and all earnings in your SMSF is still taxed at 15%. All this is, is that it allows you to withdraw funds from your SMSF/super as you come close to retirement. You are still gainfully employed and receiving salaries, but your work hours are reduced and you are receiving super benefits as well as your employment income.

- The third phase in a SMSF or super fund is called the **pension phase, or account-based pension.** This is when you have reached 60 years and retired, or are retiring, from employment, then you can commence what is called an account-based pension, and any withdrawals from this is tax-free. However, it is assumed that you still have an accumulation account because you are still employed or carrying on your business. The portion of the accumulation account in proportion to the total super balance will need to be considered in terms of tax on earnings.

Let us say that your super balance is $1 million, and your accumulation phase balance is $150,000 because you need to continue contributing or having employer contributions paid to your SMSF. The portion is 15%, and therefore any earnings will be taxed at 15% of the SMSF tax rate of 15%. E.g. if your SMSF earnings are $45,000, then the normal 15% tax is $6,750. But, given that you are now commencing an account-based pension, the majority of this is tax-free, and we call this exempt pension income. The exempt earnings portion is 85%, so essentially the tax payable is 15% on the amount of $6,750, which is $1,012.50, plus the $259 ATO Supervisory Levy. In the past, an actuarial certificate had to be provided to the SMSF and kept by you for records, but now formal actuarial certificates are not required to be provided. Your accountant/tax agent who prepares the tax return will put in the exempt pension income amount so that the tax will only be on the portion of your accumulation balance in proportion to your total super balance.

In a pension phase, the minimum withdrawal balance applies to each member, and the maximum balance you can withdraw is the total balance of your pension account. How do you determine the minimum withdrawal amount? The ATO has a table of age range and percentages, and again, we use the COVID-19 effect up until the year ended 30 June 2021 to determine the minimum percentage.

Age of recipient	Percentage Factor (2020/2021)
Under 65	2% (from 4%)
65 – 74	2.5% (from 5%)
75 – 79	3% (from 6%)
80 – 84	3.5% (from 7%)
85 – 89	4.5% (from 9%)
90 – 94	5.5% (from 11%)

95 or more   7% (from 14%)

Please note, if you fail to adhere to these minimum requirements, your SMSF will lose the account-based pension status and lose the eligibility to claim exempt pension income. This means that tax will be at 15% on all earnings in your SMSF.

Transfer balance cap

The transfer balance cap is something that the government introduced and it applies from 1 July 2017. It is a limit on the total amount of super that can be transferred into the retirement phase, or what we call pension phase.

The transfer balance cap is set at $1.6 million for the 2017–18, 2018–19 and 2019–20 income years. It is subject to indexation in line with the consumer price index (CPI), rounded down to the nearest $100,000.

You can commence multiple super income streams that are in retirement, or pension phase as long as you remain below the cap. All your super income streams that are in retirement phase are included when working out this amount. It does not matter how many accounts or funds you hold these super interests in.

The amount of indexation you are entitled to will be calculated proportionally based on the amount of your available cap space. If, at any time, you meet or exceed your cap, you will not be entitled to indexation.

Different tax rules will apply if you receive certain defined benefit income streams, known as 'capped defined benefit income streams'. You usually can't transfer or remove excess amounts from these income streams. More information on this is available from the ATO website.

Please note the transfer balance cap ONLY applies to your SMSF if you commence an account-based pension, or pension phase. It does not apply to accumulation phase accounts or transition to retirement phase accounts.

References:

ATO Website:

https://www.ato.gov.au/Individuals/Super/In-detail/Withdrawing-and-using-your-super/Withdrawing-your-super-and-paying-tax/?page=2#Transfer_balance_cap

SMSF Warehouse Website: https://www.smsfwarehouse.com.au/pensions-in-smsf/pension-phase/

Chapter 6 - Investing and taxation issues in your SMSF

Having discussed the different phases in super and in your SMSF, you can now ask the question, what are the different types of investments that your SMSF can have? There are a number of different types of investment that would allow your SMSF to comply with the SIS regulations and the ATO.

- **Equity.** This is in the form of Australian or Global shares, or units in Australian or Global managed funds. This is a fairly high-risk investment because the share market is volatile, and company shares move with the market. Managed funds are also like shares, which move up or down depending on the market movements. Global shares are more volatile and riskier, so you need to do an extensive amount of research before choosing to invest in Global Equity.
- **Real property.** This has become a very common type of investment and more SMSFs have been set up for this type of investment. Real property can be either residential or commercial (non-residential), and it can also be in the form of business real property. This is where you are running a business and your business owns the property in which it operates, there is a provision in the SIS regulations that allow transfer of business real property from the owner into the SMSF at market value. The property market may be less volatile than the share market, but you must have sufficient cash or funds to be able to purchase real property and use this as your SMSF investment.
- **Fixed Interest and cash.** This type of investment in past years was seen to be the safest investment and at one time prior to the Global Financial Crisis GFC) in 2008, the term deposit rates were as high as about 11-12%! We need to look

at reality now. The cash interest rate is now 0.25%, which is the lowest it has been in the history of Australia. The most competitive and safest term deposit rates are now around 1% p.a. and that is if you hold the cash for more than 12 months. Therefore, many SMSFs are moving away from cash and looking at other options.

- **Bonds.** This is a very interesting type of investment, simply like buying shares in the stock market. A bond, whether government, or corporate, will usually provide you with a coupon rate each year. This is like the interest rate you are receiving from investing in this bond each year. The bond has a face value of $100. Usually, the annual coupon rate will be higher than term deposit rates, and the same coupon rate will last until the bond matures. The bond value will move as the interest rates move. The coupon rate can be somewhere between 2-6% depending on the bond's policies and the bond has a maturity date, which can be over 2-8 years, or more. So if you invest in a bond and pay less than $100 per bond, then the bond will return its face value of $100, so you have made a small gain. However, in most cases, a bond's value is slightly more than face value because over the years in which the bond commenced in the market, along with changes in the interest rates, the bond increased in value. So if you bought the bond at more than $100, then you will still receive the face value of $100, but over the period of your investment, you receive the interest income from the bond, so your income over the years will likely cover the capital loss made.

- **Shares in Unlisted Public Companies.** This type of investment is still allowable in an SMSF, because it is an investment in a public company that may potentially provide you with a much better return each year than Listed Equities, real property and bonds. An SMSF cannot own shares in a private company according to the SIS regulations.

- **Units in a Fixed Unit Trust.** This is another allowable investment in an SMSF, where the SMSF buys some units in a fixed unit trust, receives income, and then can cash up and buy out all of the units and fully own the Unit Trust. It is dangerous if the Unit Trust is a related party, i.e. one of the relatives of the member/s owns a Unit Trust and your SMSF invests in this could be seen as a breach. The way out of this is that the related Unit Trust MUST own commercial or residential property for investment purposes, but such property MUST NOT be owned by a related party of your SMSF, it must be owned by a third party that is not related in any way to any of the member/s in your SMSF.

- **Collectables, artwork, jewellery.** This is another type of asset that can be purchased as part of your SMSF investment, but there are risk factors that need to be considered. If you have this type of investment, be sure that at some point, the ATO will likely review your SMSF accounts and tax return, and will ask questions as to where these assets are stored, how you came up with a market value, and so on. You do not want these headaches. Basically, it is legal for your SMSF to have this type of asset, but it must be stored in a place that is NOT owned by any member/s, or a relative of any of the members in your SMSF. Therefore, annual costs in keeping the asset safe and secure will need to be paid by your SMSF. This cost is tax deductible. You must also have a market value on this each year done by a registered valuer who is experienced in the area of collectables, artwork or jewellery. You need to conduct extensive research to determine authenticity of such type of investment so that as this increases in market value, your SMSF portfolio will also increase. Any sale of this is also subject to Capital Gains Tax provisions.

- **Mortgage Loans.** Perhaps this type of investment has started to be more common. The way this works is that you can approach a private mortgage lender, say, for example, RMBL Investments, and ask for opportunities to invest funds with them in the name of your SMSF. One of the representatives will then send you some offers at very competitive interest rates, i.e. 6-9% interest p.a. paid to your SMSF account each month. This mortgage lender offers loans for high profile property developers and construction, and the interest they charge their borrower, is what they pay you as an investor. There may be some risks involved, e.g. if the borrower cannot repay and goes broke, or if the development or construction project sinks, then you can lose some or all of your capital. There is also no guarantee of constantly receiving income - this is dependent on factors, like the borrower making their loan repayments.

- **Cryptocurrencies.** This type of investment, e.g. Bitcoin, Litecoin, Ethereum, has started to grow over years, but please, be very wary, any investment in cryptocurrencies in your SMSF will likely attract a tax office desk audit of your SMSF accounts and tax returns. This is because it is very highly volatile and you can lose some or all of your investment in a matter of weeks, depending on the market. This type of investment is treated like a capital gain when you sell, but please, do your research and determine if this fits in with the investment strategy of your SMSF.

- **Commercial storage units and car parking spaces.** This is a unique type of investment that has seen an increase of interest due to the rise of property prices and the difficulty in obtaining a loan. Storage units and car parks are much cheaper, but you need to have a look at the potential for long-term capital growth. These investments may offer you a high return each year, but the purpose of an SMSF investment is generally for a long-term capital growth. You need to also research the location of these types of investments and see if there is a capital growth potential in the location. Car park spaces can be a very, very risky investment because if there is construction work planned in the future and car park spaces are expanded or if they are taken away, then your SMSF can lose this investment and the capital amount invested. Storage units can be good investments if you have a business and need to store papers, or old business machines or items in facilities outside of your office. Your business can pay rent, **but at market rates** to your SMSF by creating a rental agreement. Like with rent on property, your business can benefit with claiming a tax deduction and saving 27.5% (or 30%) tax and your SMSF will declare rental income and be taxed at 15%. The same arrangement can be made with a car parking space.

There are other types of investments that you can make in your SMSF, but these are the main categories that I can think about, have dealt with before, and can provide some **general** information on.

Now that you have an idea about some of the different types of investments out there, you need to be aware of taxation issues of making and maintaining such investments. The most common taxation issue is capital gains, when selling a property, or an asset that is subject to the capital gains tax provisions. The concept of capital gains was introduced for assets purchased on or after 20 September 1985, and applies to most of the assets discussed in the above points. Capital gains tax does not apply to investments such as cash, fixed interest or mortgage loan investments, because these do not move up or down, and after these investments mature, you will get back your original capital.

In relation to Equity, whether Australian or Global shares, sale of this is subject to normal capital gains provisions under the taxation laws. If you held the shares or equity for less than twelve months, in fact, if you hold any asset that is subject to capital gains for less than twelve months, then the 50% discount is not available for you to use. Your capital gain will basically be sale price (proceeds) minus cost price. Brokerage fees are of-course expenses and tax deductible upon buying shares, and selling shares. Therefore, it is advisable that you hold the shares for at least twelve months before selling, that way if your SMSF made a gain, it will be able to use the 50% discount, plus the tax on the capital gain will be 10% and not 15%. The reason for this is the changes in market value at the end of the financial year gives rise to deferred tax, and any unrealised gains are not taxable until the asset is sold. The same goes for real property, bonds, units in fixed trusts, and collectables.

There are many ways in which you can invest in the share market. You can create a share trading account with a bank of your choice, and usually brokerage fees will be the most competitive and least costly when you have a share trading account with a bank. Usually the minimum purchase of shares to invest is $500.

One other way is that you can select a share trading platform that offers you access to a much wider range, but there are also many risks associated with this, as the Australian and global markets are volatile. One share trading platform that is good is BT Panorama, but the adviser and administration costs can be high, and you need to invest a minimum amount of funds and make minimum amounts of share purchases and sales. You receive monthly interest income and quarterly distributions, and shortly after the end of the financial year, your SMSF will receive an annual tax statement with the different income components. You can also contribute funds into your BT Panorama account at any time.

Real property is a type of investment that has become more popular. The next chapter will discuss borrowing arrangements and how these can work for the benefit and long-term growth of your SMSF. Like shares, property, whether residential or commercial, is subject to normal capital gains provisions under the taxation laws, and needs to be tread very carefully. Working out the cost of the property is not like working out the cost of shares, it is more than that. When you purchase property, there is stamp duty, transfer costs and other settlement costs that are not deductible, but added to the purchase price of a property. Likewise, when you sell a property in the SMSF, the sale price is included, but then you can add the selling costs to the cost of the property, e.g. commissions on sale, other settlement costs that are not deductible. Therefore, the cost base of the property can be much higher than just the purchase price, but the sale price stays the same.

Let me give an illustration. A few years ago, your SMSF purchased a property for $300,000. Stamp duty is different from state to state, but I will use Victoria as an example. The stamp duty and transfer costs on $300,000 is $13,070. Other settlement costs on purchase that your SMSF cannot claim a deduction amounts to $5,000. In this financial year, your SMSF sold the property for $600,000. So, the gain is $300,000, right? Not quite. There is commission on sale, let's say, 3% of the sale price (this usually ranges between 1% and 3%), which comes to $18,000, and other settlement costs on sale that are not deductible amounts to $5,000. The sale costs total $23,000 and the purchase costs total $18,070. Adding these two together gives you

$41,070, and that is what you add to the purchase price of $300,000, giving you a cost base for capital gains purposes of $341,070. Subtract this from the sale price of $600,000, your SMSF has a gain of $258,930. Since your SMSF held this property for more than twelve months, the effective tax on the capital gain is 10%, so it will be $25,893. Now if your SMSF is in full pension mode, which was discussed in the previous chapter, then the capital gain will be called exempt pension income, and no tax will be payable, provided your SMSF complies with the ATO and SIS regulations.

If you wish to maintain real property in your SMSF, which is advisable for long-term investment, then your SMSF declares rental income, and can claim expenses as tax deductions. This can work well if you also arrange for a Quantity Surveyor to provide a tax depreciation report. This is a document that provides an overview of the property and then outlines what your SMSF can claim in terms of depreciation on the assets in the property (Div 40 of the ITAA 97), and capital works, which is usually 2.5% p.a. on the value of the construction cost/building in the property (Div 43 of the ITAA 97). This gives your SMSF a greater deduction, in addition to the normal expenses like rates, land tax, insurance, repairs & maintenance, agent's management fees, etc. This is an effective way to minimise the tax liability in your SMSF, but regardless, your SMSF will be taxed on 15% of any earnings, but as discussed before, capital gains on assets held for more than twelve months will be effectively taxed at 10%.

If your SMSF has business real property that your business occupies, then the only deduction that the SMSF will generally claim for the property is the depreciation expense, provided it has a tax depreciation report. This is because your business will pay the outgoings in relation to occupying the premises, e.g. rates, insurance, land tax (if applicable), repairs & maintenance, etc. This way, your SMSF investment will be more effective.

The above paragraph also applies to commercial property, although there are GST considerations when your SMSF purchases commercial property. If the income from rent will be more than $75,000 p.a., then as per the ATO regulations, your SMSF must be registered for GST. If the rental income is less than $75,000, you have the option. However, if your SMSF has to pay GST on purchase of a commercial property because it is either vacant or because GST applies, your SMSF will not be able to claim the GST credits, unless it registers for GST.

Bonds, units in fixed trusts, and collectables are also subject to capital gains tax provisions. However, in relation to collectables, there are special rules around capital gains. If your SMSF purchased a collectable, e.g. artwork for less than $500, then any capital gain or loss is disregarded, so if you purchased for $499, then your SMSF does not have to report this as a capital gain or loss, regardless of how much the sale price is. However, if your SMSF purchased an artwork for $501, then it must declare a capital gain or loss. The 50% discount provisions still apply, and the effective 10% tax on the capital gain will still apply in your SMSF. For example, if your SMSF purchased artwork for $501 and sold after more than one year for $1,001, then the gain is $500, but using the 50% discount provisions, the effective tax on the gain will be $50.00 (10% of $500). However, if your SMSF, for example, purchased artwork for $900 and sold for $500, then it has a capital loss of $400. Your SMSF must declare this as a capital loss and cannot use this to offset against a capital gain from shares or property, it can only offset this against a capital gain from a collectable. This is where there is a disadvantage if your SMSF invests in collectables. There is no limit on how much capital losses from collectables can be used to carry forward. On the other hand, a capital loss from shares can be used to offset against capital gains from real property, and vice versa, but any capital losses from collectables can only be offset against capital gains from collectables.

The other taxation consideration is income derived in relation to shares, bonds, cash and investments in mortgage loans. Depending on the company and the policy of such investment, let us take for example shares in Australian listed companies, your SMSF will receive franked and unfranked dividends. Sometimes if your SMSF has Beta shares, or invests in Exchange Traded Funds (ETFs), your SMSF will receive a mix of franked and unfranked dividends. In relation to the franked dividends, the company will give your SMSF what we call 'franking credits'. This is added to your franked dividend as assessable income, but the franking credits will reduce the tax liability in your SMSF.

Let us say that your SMSF has shares as its main investment, and does not receive any contributions. Suppose the franked dividend component from the shares your SMSF receives during the financial year amount to $10,000, and the unfranked component is $3,000. The total cash dividend received is $13,000. However, the franking credit is only on $10,000, which is worked out by using the corporate tax rate ($10,000*.3/.7 for companies that pay 30% tax rate). The franking credit is $4,286 and this is added to the $13,000 dividend, which comes to $17,286. This is the taxable income of your SMSF. The tax at 15% is $2,592.90. But, the SMSF can receive a tax refund on the excess franking credit, so the refund in this case will be $1,693.10. However, there is the ATO Supervisory Levy of $259, so after subtracting this, the overall tax refund that your SMSF will receive is $1,434.10. If your SMSF is in pension mode, then the dividend plus franking credits is tax-exempt, and in this case, the franking credits amount will be refundable, less the ATO Supervisory Levy.

If your SMSF has bonds or mortgage loans as an investment, the income will usually be in the form of interest income at the rate that the bond or mortgage investment provides throughout the investment period. Interest is taxed normally at 15%.

Income tax is also payable on employer and concessional contributions, where the limit is $25,000 per year, per member. For example, if your SMSF received concessional contributions of $25,000, then this is taxed at 15%, which will be $3,750. If you are running a business in the form of a company, or if your employer is operating a company, then the company will claim a tax deduction and save 30% (or 27.5% if base rate entity) on the $25,000. Therefore, your SMSF will benefit, and your company, or employer, will also benefit from making such contributions. If your SMSF is in full pension more, then concessional contributions cannot be made. The reason is that concessional contributions is always taxed at 15% and is never tax-free. However, if your SMSF has a pension account and accumulation account, then a portion of the earnings and contributions will only be taxed, depending on the balance of your accumulation account in proportion to the total balance of your SMSF.

I want to finish off this section on the issue of in-house assets, which you would have heard before. The SIS regulations allow an SMSF to have such investment as long as the value of this is not more than 5% of the total assets of the SMSF. An example of an in-house asset is lending money to a related party from your SMSF, which is generally seen as prohibited. However, let us say that you 'accidentally' lent money to a family member or relative from your SMSF. If the value is below 5% of the SMSF total assets, that is ok, but I think your auditor will still want to report this to the ATO and state that you have rectified this the moment it was brought to your attention. Perhaps you paid off a tax debt for your business out of your SMSF. As long as it is less than 5% of the total assets in your SMSF, that is ok provided that you rectify the situation and have the business pay back your SMSF as quickly and practicably as possible. At the end of the day, any of the above transactions must be declared in the SMSF Annual Return as an in-house asset.

Chapter 7 - Borrowing in your SMSF

Having discussed some taxation aspects and touched on real property in the previous chapter, this section presents a further discussion on borrowing provisions and how to borrow in order to grow your SMSF for the long-term. In the past, before 2007 an SMSF was absolutely prohibited from borrowing and there was no arrangement in place as we have now. So, if your SMSF had a Trust Deed before 2007, chances are that the Deed has no provision for borrowing. In fact, the Deed will likely state that the SMSF cannot borrow. The reality is that an SMSF is not allowed to borrow, except under certain specific circumstances. Therefore, you need to update your SMSF Trust Deed so that it will allow for the new borrowing provisions. Since the ATO introduced regulations and provisions around Limited Recourse Borrowing Arrangements (LRBAs), there have been updates, improvements and further limitations in these provisions almost every year.

Firstly, if you are considering borrowing in your SMSF, you need to include this in the investment strategy (discussed in chapter 4) and explain how the borrowing will benefit your SMSF in the long-term, outline the risks associated with the borrowing, and how the risk may be overcome, i.e. that the rental income will cover the interest and loan repayments each month. The reason for mentioning this is because borrowing is a long-term commitment and should be tread very carefully.

There are extra costs associated with borrowing in your SMSF. You need to set up a Custodian Trust (also known as a Bare Trust) along with a Corporate/Company Trustee for the Bare Trust. This is because your SMSF itself will not be the direct borrower, but it will be the Bare Trust of your SMSF. Yes, the property will be in the name of your SMSF and your SMSF will make the loan repayments, but the Bare Trust is the legal owner of the property.

These are the components in relation to borrowing in an SMSF:

- The lender is a third-party (external) entity, e.g. bank or other private lender, or it could be a related party, i.e. your company.
- The borrower is your SMSF and the SMSF receives the income from the property, and makes the loan repayments.
- The Bare Trust of your SMSF is a Custodian and the 'legal' owner, or the 'real landlord' of the property, until the loan is paid off.

Let us say that you have ABC Pty Ltd as trustee for ABC Superannuation Fund. You will need to set up another trust, the Bare Trust with a Company Trustee, for example you can have ABC Bare Pty Ltd as trustee for ABC Superannuation Fund Bare. This is the Trust that will borrow the funds from the third-party lender. Please note also that ABC Bare Pty Ltd is to be registered as a regular company, and therefore the annual ASIC fees for this is currently around $273. It can cost up to another $1,000 to $2,000 to set up the Bare Trust, but if you do it yourself, you can use the steps in chapter 2 but rather than starting an SMSF, you need to create a Bare Trust Deed with an External Lender, and with a Corporate Trustee. In relation to the Corporate Trustee of the Bare Trust, it is advisable and recommended that you have the same member/s as in your SMSF (ABC Superannuation Fund) and the same director/s and shareholder/s as in the trustee Company of your SMSF (ABC Pty

Ltd). This minimises the confusions of having two trusts and two companies with different people and different names.

The Bare Trust Deed has to include the following details when creating it for the purpose of borrowing:

- Name and details of the lender
- Name and details of the borrower
- Address of the property
- Loan amount and the interest rate (if this is a related-party borrowing arrangement)
- The term of the loan (if this is a related-party borrowing arrangement)

Now that you have the details, you can set up the Bare Trust Deed, and after it has been set up you will receive all the legal paperwork in relation to the Limited Recourse Borrowing Arrangement (LRBA) and the terms of the loan. Again, setting this up is a matter of minutes, just like setting up your SMSF.

The borrowing arrangement works really good especially if you have a business and want to purchase an office, or another commercial property in the name of your SMSF. You take a loan and then your business pays to your SMSF the rent amounts, but it MUST be at market rates, not below, or above, because it will be seen as taking advantage of the situation, and this will breach the SIS regulations. Any breach of the SIS regulations, depending on the seriousness of the issue, results in the income and asset being non-arms' length transaction, i.e. the transaction is not a market rate, and therefore your SMSF will be taxed at 45%, both the income and the asset in question.

Now that you are aware of some of the implications, let us say that your business occupies an office in your SMSF, which is under a LRBA. The trustee of the Bare Trust of your SMSF is the landlord, but your SMSF receives rent income from your business. Generally, your business will pay the outgoings of the office, so that it provides your SMSF with more cash flow in order to pay off the loan and other obligations, e.g. pensions if applicable. The interest expense on the loan is tax deductible and is an effective way to reduce your SMSF tax liability. However, it is not advisable that your SMSF will continue making tax losses as a result because a tax loss reduces the balance of your SMSF and you may not have sufficient cash available on retirement. Therefore, if this is your only asset in the SMSF and the interest on loan generates a tax loss, then it may not be worthwhile to take a loan in the form of a LRBA.

How can your SMSF enter into a LRBA? One way is through a bank, although the big four banks like CBA, Westpac, NAB and ANZ all withdrew from lending to SMSFs, regardless of the SMSF account balance and the fact that it has sufficient cash to cover the loan. However, it is not the end of the world, as the Bank of Queensland and Macquarie, just to name a few banks, along with some other private lenders, can still lent to SMSFs, but the interest rates are higher, there is also a minimum loan amount for borrowing, and the lenders may provide anywhere between 50-80% of the total purchase cost of the property, depending on where you go. Please note also that the interest rates can be quite high, going up to around 6-7%, so you need to shop around for competitive rates. In order to enter into this kind of arrangement, you will need to set up a Bare Trust Deed with an external lender, i.e. bank or private lending institution, and these must have an Australian Financial Services and credit license. There are set up costs, so it is up to you whether you want to engage an accountant, or set it up yourself, you will still pay some costs.

However, the ATO has guidelines for banks in terms of lending to SMSFs, like how much a minimum balance the SMSF must have before the bank considers to lend. Now there is no law that states your SMSF must have a particular balance, but in order to take advantage of a LRBA with a bank, the ATO has strict guidelines for the remaining banks that provide lending to SMSFs. You may like to check on the ATO website and with the bank on these guidelines. Perhaps a private lender with a financial services and credit license may not be bound by the ATO guidelines, but please, do your research and check.

If for some reason or another the bank or external lender does not provide your SMSF with a borrowing, the other form of a LRBA is through a related party. For example, your business/company may have cash reserves and is prepared to lend to your SMSF. You must seek professional advice before thinking of that, but this can be done, by setting up a Bare Trust Deed with a related party, which will cost more money to set up because the LRBA will be done through a related party. In this case, the related party, i.e. your company, will be the lender and legal owner of the property, and your SMSF is the borrower. It is absolutely a MUST, that the interest rate is at the market rates that are offered by other commercial property lenders, you cannot just have your company offer a lower interest rate, that is a NO NO! If this happens, you must rectify the situation immediately, otherwise your SMSF will face significant penalties and fines, depending on the issue and you as the trustee, or director of the trustee Company will be liable. If this is done properly, and suppose that your business will occupy the property in the SMSF, then you both will benefit, but the rent returns must be at market rates. Your business pays rent each month to your SMSF, resulting in your business claiming a tax deduction, saving 30% tax (or 27.5% if base rate entity) and your SMSF will pay 15% tax on the earnings. This provides a combined tax saving of 15%. Subsequently, your SMSF will make loan repayments including interest, to your company, so your SMSF will claim a deduction for the interest, and in turn the interest component of the loan repayment is assessable to your company, and normal company tax rates apply. This is just a scenario if your business occupies the property that your SMSF will have under the LRBA with a related party.

Perhaps your SMSF property already has a tenant. If this is the case, then rent will also be at market rates, and therefore, your SMSF will still have to make the loan repayments to your company under the LRBA with the related party loan, using the market rates for working out the interest component.

Once you have the borrowing approved and set up the Bare Trust Deed (can also be known as Declaration of Custody Trust), depending on the state in Australia where your property investment is, the Bare Trust Deed is required to be stamped by the relevant revenue office, or at least a certificate of stamping may be a minimum requirement. This can be done by engaging competent solicitors, or by using a website service that is suited to the state where your SMSF investment property is located. You will need to register online and create a password if doing this by yourself. You will need to lodge a Declaration of Trust (NOT Declaration of Custody Trust) and pay for the stamping. Please consult with your professional accountant or solicitor for more accurate and specific advice.

When your SMSF has paid off the loan, then the Custodian Trustee will transfer legal ownership of the property to your SMSF Trustee, and discharge of loan documents will need to be prepared. This means that the Custodian (Bare) Trust is no longer the legal owner of the property, and as a result, the Bare Trust can be wound up and the Bare Trustee Company can be deregistered. This is done in the same way as a company deregistration and winding up a trust. Your accountant/tax agent will likely do this for you at an extra cost. As always, you can also do this by yourself if you wish to save costs. There are helpful guides on deregistering a company and winding up of trust. Usually when you set up a Bare Trust for your SMSF through a service provider online, there may be an option where you can wind up the Bare Trust.

Chapter 8 - Taxation on Super Pensions & Death Benefits

This section now covers the different taxation treatments of pension payments, and also payments in relation to death benefits. There are regulations from the ATO on these issues which will be discussed at length. If you receive a pension earlier than retirement age on compassionate grounds, chances are that you will be taxed on this at your marginal tax rate. Furthermore, if you receive a death benefit (this is when a member of the SMSF is deceased), you will be taxed depending on whether you are a dependant for super and tax purposes. This chapter will cover situations and examples on what tax amounts are payable and what is not payable upon receipt of funds or benefits.

You should know at this stage that you cannot withdraw from your SMSF before reaching preservation age unless under certain circumstances as outlined on the ATO website.

As a result of the COVID-19 pandemic, you are allowed to withdraw up to $10,000 in the 2020-21 financial year, tax-free. This means you don't need to declare this in your individual tax return. However, you must meet criteria that is in place by the ATO, and the tax office must be satisfied that you have been heavily affected as a result of the pandemic. Some of the criteria include a significant loss of income, loss of your employment, and other factors that need to be satisfied before making a tax-free withdrawal. The ATO has made it clear that if you withdraw from super, and do not meet the criteria, depending on the circumstances, the ATO may penalise you. In addition, you must include the withdrawal as assessable income in your individual tax return. The ATO have measures in place and they check withdrawals from super in relation to the COVID-19 situation.

Let us say that you withdrew funds from your SMSF based on the compassionate grounds as set out by the ATO. The tax-free component of the balance that you withdraw will always be tax-free, regardless of your age or how you withdraw the money. However, there is some tax that you have to pay upon withdrawal. Let's say for example that you withdrew $40,000 and the tax-free component is $20,000. You will need to declare in your tax return assessable income of $20,000 because this is the taxable component. Usually, the taxable component will be from a taxed element, and if you take this $20,000 as a lump sum, then the tax rate on this amount is your marginal tax rate including the Medicare Levy, or 22%, whichever is lower. Suppose your income is around $38,000. This means that the tax bracket of your marginal rate is 32.5%. However, the tax on the $20,000 withdrawal will be 22%.

What if you took the $40,000 as an income stream? Well, the tax-free component will always be tax-free, so there will be tax on $20,000. The tax on this is your marginal rate of tax including Medicare Levy. However, if you received this income stream as a disability super benefit, you will be entitled to a 15% tax offset on the $20,000, so an offset of $3,000. This offset reduces your tax liability by $3,000. However, your super (or SMSF) will also have to withhold a certain amount of money from you because you are under 60. This is called Pay As You Go (PAYG) Withholding and you can include this as PAYG credit in your tax return. You will receive a payment summary from your super (or SMSF) showing the gross amount and the PAYG tax. Information on this is available on the ATO website and your accountant will know how to prepare this payment summary.

The next age range is when you are between preservation age and 60 years old. Previously in the section of the different phases in super and in your SMSF, if you were born on or after 1 July 1964, then your preservation age will be 60. If you were born before 1 July 1960, then you will have reached your preservation age of 55. If you were born between 1 July 1960 and 30 June 1964, then your preservation age is different. The age table is in chapter 5.

Let us say that you have reached preservation age, and you wish to know how much tax you need to pay after withdrawing from your SMSF. You have two options.

The first option is to withdraw a lump sum (one-off withdrawal in the financial year), up to the low rate cap of $210,000 for the 2019-20 financial year, and $215,000 for the 2020-21 financial year. If you withdraw anywhere up to that amount, then it is all tax-free and you do not need to declare this in your tax return. However, if you are desperate for money and need to withdraw above the low rate cap, then tax is payable on the excess. Let us say that you withdraw

$250,000 lump sum in the 2019-20 financial year. The excess is $40,000. You must still declare the amount of $250,000 in your tax return (but state that it is a lump sum), and pay marginal tax rate including Medicare Levy, or 17%, whichever is lower. Let's say that your other source of income is $30,000. This puts you in the tax bracket, including Medicare Levy, of 21% (19% plus 2% Medicare Levy). However, the tax on the $40,000 excess will be 17%, which is $6,800 because this is lower than your marginal tax rate.

The second option is to take an income stream. This will attract PAYG Withholding, and guidance is available on the ATO website on the rates of PAYG to include on the income stream. Basically, the tax-free component of any withdrawal is always tax-free, so we are looking at the taxable component. Let us say that you take an income stream of $60,000 and this is all taxable component of your super balance. There is no low rate cap, because you are taking an income stream, so this cap is not available. The tax on $60,000 is your marginal rate including Medicare Levy, less a 15% tax offset. A simple exercise, le us say that you have $40,000 other source of income and then you take a super income stream of $60,000. You will then be in the 37% tax bracket, so your marginal tax will be 39% (37% plus 2% Medicare Levy). Tax on the $60,000 income stream will be $23,400 but a 15% offset of $9,000 will be available. Therefore, the net tax payable on this income stream will be $14,400 ($23,400 less $9,000).

Income tax will be treated differently if you are in receipt of a defined benefit income stream, which is not very common these days. More information is available on the ATO website, and you can also engage your accountant on more details on defined benefit income streams.

The last age range is for those who have reached 60 and over. Any withdrawal amounts, whether lump sum, income stream, taxed element, is all tax-free and not included in your tax return. Therefore, if you are not desperate for money if you are at preservation age or below, you can wait until retirement age, reduce your work/business hours and take any amounts from super tax-free.

I need to mention a note about the tax-free components and taxable components in your super balance. This is a percentage, and not just a random number. Let us say you have a super balance of $100,000 and the tax-free component is $30,000. The taxable component is $70,000. The percentages are 30% tax-free and 70% taxable. Now let us say you withdraw $30,000. Please be aware, this is NOT all tax-free. We MUST use the percentage that is worked out. The tax-free percentage of the $30,000 is still 30%, so the tax-free amount of this withdrawal is $9,000 and the remaining $21,000 is the taxable amount.

The other type of benefit that you can receive is a death benefit, when a member is deceased and there are dependants. This type of benefit is taxed differently and treated differently than a regular super payment. The tax on the death benefit is dependent on whether you were a dependant of the deceased, whether it is paid as a lump sum or income stream, whether the income stream is account based or a capped defined benefit income stream, the tax-free and taxable components of the super amount, and your age and the age of the deceased when they died. All these factors are taken into account to determine the tax payable on receipt of a death benefit.

If you are a dependant of the deceased for tax purposes and receive the benefit as a lump sum, there is no tax payable on this. If the benefit is via income stream, different tax rates may apply based on the factors in the above paragraph. If you are not a dependant of the deceased, then you can only receive the benefit as a lump sum, and tax on the benefit is only on the taxed element, a maximum of 15% plus Medicare Levy. Let us say that you are not a dependant and received $50,000 lump sum death benefit. $20,000 of this is the tax-free component, so you will pay 17% tax (15% plus 2% Medicare Levy) on $30,000, which is $5,100.

The ATO has information on who is a dependant for super purposes and a dependant for tax purposes of the deceased, and usually age ranges and circumstances of the individual, family ties and other factors are used for the ATO to determine whether you are a dependant of the deceased for tax or super purposes.

In the event of a death benefit, the trustee/s look at the concept of whether the deceased has made a binding or non-binding death nomination. This is crucial as the benefit may fall into hands of recipients that were not initially targeted. More information on binding nominations and how these can be done is available online, and you can also speak with your accountant or solicitor about setting up a will with a binding death nomination. In summary, a binding death benefit nomination is "a legally binding nomination that allows you to advise the trustee who is to receive your superannuation benefit in the event of your death. In order for a nomination to be binding, it must be 'valid'. One of the requirements of validity is that only 'dependants' can be nominated. Depending on your circumstances, however, you can nominate one dependant or a number of dependants. For the purposes of superannuation law, a dependant includes:

- a spouse (including de facto, opposite and same-sex)
- children of any age (including adopted or ex-nuptial)
- any person(s) financially dependent on the member
- any person(s) in an interdependency relationship with the member (applicable since 1 July 2004)
- a legal personal representative (LPR)".

One of the biggest benefits you receive from having a binding death benefit nomination in place is peace of mind. This is especially the case if you have multiple beneficiaries (eg from previous marriages) who may have a claim on your death benefit.

In this case, you can nominate with reasonable certainty who you wish to receive your death benefit or, if being paid to more than one beneficiary, who receives what proportion.

Another advantage of a binding death benefit nomination is the ease and speed with which a death benefit can be paid.

If your beneficiary needs quick access to your benefit, a binding death benefit nomination may allow a timelier distribution of your assets and your beneficiary won't have to wait for the trustee or the deceased estate to determine the distribution.

A non-binding nomination, on the other hand, gives the trustee discretion to protect the interests of your beneficiaries if circumstances change. For example, if one of your beneficiaries is bankrupt, the trustee can take this into account and avoid putting your super benefit into the hands of creditors instead of your beneficiaries.

References:

Bridges:
https://www.bridges.com.au/pdf_flyers/ed_flyers/superannuation/what_is_a_binding_death_benefit_nomination#:~:text=Put%20simply%2C%20a%20binding%20death,the%20event%20of%20your%20death.&text=Depending%20on%20your%20circumstances%2C%20however,or%20a%20number%20of%20dependants.

Shadforth Financial Group:

https://www.sfg.com.au/education_tools/education_guides/education_flyers/superannuation_flyers/what_is_a_binding_death_benefit_nomination#:~:text=A%20binding%20death%20benefit%20nomination%20is%20a%20way%20to%20override,the%20event%20of%20your%20death.

Chapter 9 - Annual financial accounts and the audit report

Having discussed the major components of your SMSF and types of investments you can make, we now come to the annual financial accounts and audit report of your SMSF. Your accountant or tax agent will prepare the annual accounts and usually the audit report will be attached with the accounts, but signed by an independent, ASIC approved registered SMSF auditor.

It is absolutely vital to obtain all the source documents of your SMSF investment from the beginning to end of the financial year, because this is how the accounts, or financial statements, are produced and generated. The most important item is the bank statements for the whole financial year. If you have shares in your SMSF portfolio, then your broker, or whichever bank you have a share trading account with, will send you a portfolio statement shortly after the end of the financial year. This is vital because the SMSF financial report must reconcile the number of shares and the **market value** of shares or units in each company back to the portfolio holdings as at the end of the financial year. The SMSF must also have a reconciliation of income, i.e. interest and dividends from your share trading account for the financial year.

Some of the expenses that you need to include in your SMSF are accountancy fees, bank charges (where applicable), ASIC fees if the trustee is a Company, auditor's remuneration, ATO Supervisory Levy (if this is an existing fund, then the tax paid from the previous financial year will also have the Supervisory Levy). Other expenses include advisor fees or administration costs if you have a share trading account with a platform like BT Panorama, or if you have investment in First Choice, your annual tax summary will include these types of fees that you can claim in your SMSF as a deduction.

The bank account balances must reconcile back to the actual bank statements, and if the figure is different, there may be a deposit or cheque that has not cleared until after the end of the financial year. Records must be kept in working out these differences.

If your SMSF has real property, whether residential or commercial property, the following documents must be kept and provided to your accountant for timely and accurate preparation of the financial statements: a statement from the agent, if your SMSF engaged an agent, this will be an annual statement showing the total rent received, expenses paid by the agent, and the net amounts received, which should tally back to the bank statement deposits. Extra expenses and documents that need to be kept include any outgoings paid relating to the investment property, e.g. council rates, land tax assessments, water rates, insurance/body corporate invoices, repairs & maintenance and any other expenses. The rent income and agent commissions, and expenses paid by the agent, must reconcile back to the agent statement.

If you have a loan on the property, the accountant and auditor will need to see the Custodian (Bare) Trust Deed, and loan agreement to verify that the transactions are at market rates and that there is no breach in the SIS regulations. You will also need the loan statements which include the total interest paid and any bank charges on the loan account. The loan account balance in the SMSF balance sheet must reconcile with the actual statement. Interest and bank fees on the loan are tax deductible, so it is vital that you have this record.

If you purchased or sold property during the financial year, then purchase, sale contracts and settlement statements must be provided to the accountant to correctly enter the capital gain/loss on sale, or to record the purchase price of the property correctly in the accounts. Your accountant and independent auditor will also request a market valuation of your property, which can be provided in a letter by a real estate agent or a registered valuer. The market valuation will be between a low and a high range, so the accountant will use their professional judgement to enter a market value of the property with the supporting valuation. If you have a tax depreciation report from a Quantity Surveyor, you need to provide this to your accountant so that they can correctly allocate depreciation expense on the property.

The other very important record you need is the contributions made to your SMSF for the financial year. If there is more than one member, you need to reconcile the contributions for each member to what the employer/s have paid into your SMSF. This is absolutely vital because concessional contributions are capped at $25,000 for each member, and if you made more than $25,000 contributions, the excess will be allocated as non-concessional (non-deductible) contributions.

If you had balances from other super funds and rolled over to your SMSF during the financial year, you need to have the rollover benefits statement from your other super fund/s, with the tax-free and taxable components that must be included when entering the deposit of the rollover amount.

If your SMSF is in transition to retirement, or pension mode, then you must reconcile pension payments to members with the bank statements. Payment summaries must be issued to each member showing the total amount paid during the financial year. In the past, actuarial certificates were required to determine the exempt pension income portion, but now it is not required. A manual actuarial certificate can be produced from most SMSF software providers.

As part of the SMSF financials, the member statement is a vital component. This should include the opening balance, any contributions received, whether concessional, non-concessional, spouse, ATO co-contributions, in-specie contributions, all need to be added to the opening balance. The next item is any earnings or losses to be allocated, plus any income tax for each member to be allocated properly and shown separately in each member statement. If there are any rollovers, this must also be shown separately, and is an addition to the member balance. Pension payments need to be taken into account, so if any member receives a pension, or a death benefit, this needs to be deducted from the member's balance, and supporting documents must be kept. After all these components, the closing balance of the member's account is calculated, and in the statement, the member's name, date of birth, address and age must be shown. The tax-free component and taxable components must also be clearly shown in the member's statement.

After using the source documents to generate the financial statements, the profit and tax allocations to each member is usually done based on the member's portion of the total super balance. The financials will have a change in market value in the income statement, which is not taxed until the asset or investment is actually sold. The balance sheet will show an income tax payable amount, which is 15% of the taxable income, not the accounting profit. This amount is without the Supervisory Levy, which will be included in the next financial year after the tax is paid. As you are aware, the tax is calculated on the concessional contributions and the earnings (income minus expenses). If there is a change in market value and your SMSF still has the investment/s, there will be a deferred tax asset/liability in the balance sheet of the SMSF.

All in all, your SMSF income, expenses, assets and liabilities must reconcile back to the source documents, because the auditor will have to prepare the report whether or not the accounts presenting a true and fair view of the financial position and performance of the SMSF. If there is not sufficient evidence, then your auditor will give you an opportunity to supply the documents, or your SMSF audit report will either be a qualified report or an 'inability to form an opinion' report.

At the end of the day, there should not be any discrepancies in the financial report. However, if you have used any funds from the

SMSF for private purposes, or if you withdrew from the SMSF without any compassionate grounds or evidence, then the auditor must be informed and use their professional judgement to form an opinion on part B of the audit report, which is the compliance section. If the withdrawal or private use (which is called an in-house asset discussed earlier) is less than 5% of the fund's total assets, then that is ok, but the trustee (member) must repay the funds back to the SMSF.

Once the auditor is satisfied that source documents have been sighted and used to generate the financial statements and that no discrepancies exist, the auditor will prepare a report, which is basically called SMSF audit report. The auditor will provide their opinion of part A and B of the financial report, and will issue an unqualified opinion. This is actually a good opinion in audit terms, whereas a qualified opinion is not a good opinion. The unqualified opinion will generally be in the form of wordings that the financial report presents fairly, in all material respects, in accordance with accounting policies described in the notes to the financial statements. This is part A of the audit report; and that each trustee of the SMSF has complied, in all material respects, with the applicable provisions of the SIS Act and Superannuation Regulations, which is part B of the audit report.

If there has been big mistake, i.e. you withdrew or provided financial assistance from your SMSF to a member or relative, and the amount is more than 5% of the fund's total assets, then your auditor must be informed and then will likely issue a qualified opinion in the compliance section of the audit report. The auditor will mention what happened and state the nature of the event. Depending on the amount and nature, the auditor will likely lodge an Auditor's Contravention Report (ACR) to the ATO. It is vital at this stage that you plan to, or even repay any amounts within a certain timeframe (probably 28 days) after this event has been made aware to you and the auditor. The auditor will then note this in the ACR that the breach has been rectified and the funds have been repaid back to the SMSF, or will be repaid back within a reasonable time period after lodging the ACR. These things are very serious, because it may lead the SMSF to become unsatisfactory especially if the transactions are repeated and the trustee is aware that they are doing the wrong thing. The trustee may also be penalised and the SMSF will be taxed at 45% and lose the complying status.

In concluding this chapter, records, source documents and everything relating to the SMSF must be kept for a period of 10 years according to the law. These documents include bank statements, pension payments and summaries, portfolio holdings statements, property contracts and rental agent statements, rental agreements (where applicable), market valuation reports, loan statements and interest components, super rollover benefits statements, ASIC statements relating to the trustee company, Trust Deed, and Custodian (Bare) Trust Deed (if applicable). This is not an exhaustive list, but is a minimum requirement for documents that must be kept. There is no-where in the law that prescribes you must keep physical papers as proper records. It can be a simple matter of keeping the files stored on your computer or a hard drive and ensure these are in order of financial year to make it simpler for you to go back to the documents when required. Of-course, the financial statements, auditor's report and the SMSF Annual Return must also be kept.

Chapter 10 - The SMSF Annual Tax Return

After preparing the financial statements and audit report, the document that is lodged and submitted to the ATO is called the SMSF Annual Return. This is required to be lodged by the due date, which is usually at the end of October after the relevant financial year. If you have a tax agent and your SMSF lodgements are on time, your SMSF Return will be due sometime in May the following year. For example, your SMSF Annual Return 2020 will be due sometime in May 2021. Even if you lodge early, any tax payable will still be due on the date as set out by the ATO.

A paper tax return can be downloaded from the ATO website by typing the following link, or searching the ATO site for NAT 71226, which is the form called Self-managed superannuation fund annual return 2020.

https://www.ato.gov.au/uploadedFiles/Content/IND/Downloads/Self-managed-superannuation-fund-annual-return-2020.pdf

In order to complete the SMSF annual return, you need to have all the details of your SMSF filled properly. The different sections in the SMSF Annual Return are:

Section A: SMSF Information

- Name of the SMSF
- TFN
- ABN
- Trustee, whether company or individual, and name of the trustee
- Address of the SMSF
- Bank account details - account name, BSB and account number
- Whether the fund commenced or is being wound up during the year
- The type of the fund
- Date the audit report was completed
- Name of the SMSF auditor, address and auditor registration number
- Whether part A and part B of the audit report was qualified or not
- Whether there was any pension paid during the year

Section B: Income

Having filled these details, you then need to transfer the income from the financial statements, namely the income statement, and use the figures in the tax return. This guide is if you are doing it by yourself and not engaging an accountant to prepare the tax return for you. Even if you are doing it by yourself, you must have an approved auditor's details and notify the auditor that you are preparing the financials and tax return by yourself. However, it is recommended that you leave this to your professional accountant/tax agent, because chances are that the software used to prepare SMSF financial accounts and audit report will also integrate the figures into the tax return and cut the work by almost half.

The income components in the tax return are:

- Interest, including TFN withholding
- Dividends, both franked and unfranked, along with franking credits
- Distributions received, including from Family Trusts
- Foreign income and tax credits
- Rental income
- Capital gains event - you must tick yes when the question asks if you had a capital gains event, if you sold any assets subject to CGT, even if it was sold at a loss. The components are current year gains and net capital gain. If you made a capital gain using the discount method and the 10% concession (if you held the asset for at least 12 months) then the net capital gain will be less than the current year gain, and the net gain will be taxed at 10%.
- Contributions - concessional and non-concessional. Remember, the concessional contributions received in the SMSF is taxed at 15%.
- Non-arms' length income - this is where the SMSF is seen to be non-complying and any income is taxed at 45%. One of the reasons it may be non-complying is that the SMSF paid less than the minimum percentage of pension payments that it has to pay to a member who is receiving retirement phase superannuation benefits.

Section C: Deductions and non-deductible expenses

The next section is the expenses section. This includes administration costs, auditor's remuneration, depreciation, and all other expenses that the SMSF incurred during the year. This can be transferred from the expenses section in the Income Statement, but any pension payments do not belong in the tax return under expenses. Generally, SMSFs that derive exempt pension income cannot claim a deduction for expenses incurred in respect to that income. For example, if your SMSF exempt pension income is 85%, then 85% of the expenses will not be deductible. You cannot incur a tax loss in that way.

Having entered the income and expenses information, the tax return calculates the taxable income or loss. If it is a loss, then the small box underneath the word 'loss' is ticked to indicate that the SMSF has incurred a tax loss for the financial year.

Section D: Income tax calculation statement

This section calculates the income tax payable if there is a taxable income figure from section C. This figure is transferred to section D and a prima-facie 15% tax expense is calculated automatically. There may be adjustments if the SMSF has franking credits, TFN Withholding credits, foreign tax credits, etc. If your accountant prepares the financial accounts and tax return, these will automatically be included. If you are preparing the tax return by yourself, you will need to rely on a software package to reduce your input time, otherwise you will have to manually write the figures in the tax return on paper. After working out all the tax offsets, you then need to consider if there are any PAYG Income Tax Instalment payments during the year. This will come from the Quarterly PAYG Instalment Notices that the ATO sends to SMSF trustees. After entering this amount, you then enter the ATO Supervisory Levy of $259.00 (if you are manually inputting these on paper), and then you come to an overall income tax payable or refund.

The SMSF can have a refund where there are excess franking credits, or where the tax instalments were more than the actual tax liability, or both. Please note that a complying SMSF is entitled to a refund if it is unable to fully utilise the tax offset in reducing its income tax whereas a non-complying SMSF is not entitled a refund of the unused portion of a tax offset amount.

Section E: Losses

This section calculates any tax losses or capital losses carried forward. If you are preparing the tax return by yourself on paper, this can get a bit tricky because you need a record of the prior year tax and/or capital losses, and then apply any income or loss in the section. A tax software will automatically include prior year losses from the first time the loss occurred, and will apply additional losses or offset any income against the losses in future years. The losses figure for tax and/or capital losses represents the loss that is to be carried forward to future years.

Sections F and G: Member information and Supplementary member information

This is where you include details of each member. Personal details, TFN and date of birth of the members need to be included. The opening balances of each member account must be included in this section before commencing on other components. Rollovers and transfers-in, contributions, including concessional, non-concessional, government co-contribution, spouse, in-specie, all need to be allocated to their appropriate labels. The next item is to include any earnings or losses to the member's account, along with the income tax allocation. After that any benefits paid and rollover/transfers-out will need to be included. Where the SMSF paid benefits, there are codes in relation to the benefits paid, and you need to determine the type of benefit, and whether it was paid as a lump sum or income stream. Having included all this information, the closing balance of each member can then be calculated. This must reconcile back to the financial report and the member statements attached to the financial report.

If a member is in retirement phase, you also need to include the number of retirement phase accounts for each member in this section.

In section G, include any member who left the fund during the financial year in which the tax return is being lodged, i.e. 2019-20. In section G, include anyone who was a member of the SMSF at any time during 2019-20, but is not a member on 30 June 2020. This could include:

- deceased members (even if there was money in their account on 30 June 2020)
- former members who left the SMSF by rolling out all their benefits
- former members who left the SMSF by being paid all of their benefits as a super lump sum or the final payment of an income stream.

If the SMSF has more than four members on 30 June 2020:

- it has breached superannuation law. You can have only up to four members.
- in section G include the members whom you cannot include in section F due to lack of space.

Section H: Assets and Liabilities

Include in this section the fund's assets and liabilities by classification. This includes assets such as Australian managed investments (managed funds), Australian direct investments (shares, real property), other investments, overseas direct investments (shares, real property), in-house assets, limited recourse borrowing arrangements (LRBA), and liabilities. In the assets section, you need to separately include cash assets (this includes term deposits), and other assets like crypto-currency (if applicable).

In relation to LRBA, any asset value that has a borrowing against it, such as property, the market value of this asset must be included in the LRBA section, and a property count must be provided, i.e. number of properties under a LRBA. You need to answer the question whether the borrowing was from a licenced financial institution, and whether members or related parties used personal guarantees or other security for the LRBA. For the first question, you can answer no if the LRBA was from a related party.

The liabilities section includes borrowings, but you need to enter the borrowing amount under borrowings under a limited recourse borrowing arrangement. This includes the outstanding loan balance subject to the LRBA. Please do not put this under 'other liabilities'. The section of other liabilities should include the tax payable amounts, or sundry creditors, which is basically if there is a quarterly tax instalment payable related to April to June 2020.

Section I: Taxation of financial arrangements

This section is whether the taxation of financial arrangements provisions apply to the SMSF. Please see your professional accountant/tax agent for help on this section if you are unsure.

Section J: Other information

Complete this section if the SMSF has made or is making a family trust election or an interposed entity election. Again, if you are unsure about this section, please see your professional accountant/tax agent.

Section K: Declarations

In this section, you need to declare that you have met your obligations as trustee of the SMSF in relation to the annual return. You, as the trustee, or the director of the trustee company, need to sign this section and your tax agent will also need to declare and sign this section.

You can see that it can be very tricky if you have a number of investments and LRBA, if you are going to prepare the annual return by yourself, especially if on paper, it can be very tedious. Even if you have good software package that prepares SMSF financial statements and annual returns, it can be time consuming if you are not very skilled with numbers and sections. For this reason, it is recommended that you see a professional accountant/tax agent to prepare your SMSF affairs, and negotiate a reasonable cost to tailor your needs and requirements. However, it is your duty as trustee, or as the director of the company trustee, to keep records and be clean in your SMSF affairs.

References:

ATO website instructions for SMSF Annual Return: https://www.ato.gov.au/Forms/Self-managed-superannuation-fund-annual-return-instructions-2020/

Chapter 11 - Winding up your SMSF

One of the common reasons that an SMSF will be wound up is that it has ceased its purpose. It may be that the fund has sold all its assets and paid all available pensions and benefits to its members, and therefore the sole purpose test is no longer required. One other reason may be that the trustee/s have decided that the SMSF is not providing the intended returns expected for the member/s, and chose to rollover their benefits in the SMSF to an APRA-regulated super fund in order to benefit more from the large funds. Perhaps the trustee/s decided that it is too much work and efforts, and it may be more risky to manage a SMSF and decide that the best course of action is to move to an APRA-regulated fund. Another reason can be that it was found out the SMSF has breached multiple regulations of the SIS Act and the ATO, and it has been forced to wind up and the trustee/s may be disqualified from managing and maintaining a SMSF in the future. These are some reasons why SMSFs are wound up and closed. This last chapter will discuss how to wind up or close your SMSF if you wish to do most of the work and just involve an accountant or solicitor to initiate the final step.

As per the ATO requirements, before winding up your SMSF, you need to:

- complete any requirements that the trust deed specifies about winding up the fund. This will be outlined in the section of the trust deed that has information about winding up your SMSF.
- pay out or rollover all super (leaving a sufficient amount to pay final tax or expenses if required).
- appoint an SMSF auditor to complete the final audit - this may be your regular SMSF auditor.
- complete and lodge a final SMSF annual return (including wind up details). You need to select in the annual return that this is a final return and is being wound up during the year.
- pay any outstanding tax.
- after all expected liabilities have been settled and requested refunds are received, close the fund's bank account.

Once a fund is wound up, it cannot be reactivated. When you wind up your SMSF and pay benefits to the member/s, they must meet a condition of release allowing them to access their benefits, i.e. they must be at preservation or retirement age. If they don't meet this condition or don't want to access their benefits when the fund winds up, you can roll over the benefits to an APRA-regulated fund, or another complying super fund. There are serious penalties for accessing your super before you are legally allowed, which includes possibility of disqualification as a trustee and the SMSF being taxed at 45% and losing the complying status.

There may be capital gains tax (CGT) implications for your SMSF on sale or disposal of assets to enable the payment of benefits or the rollover of benefits to another fund, so this needs to be considered when leaving some amounts for tax liability.

If one or more of your members are in retirement phase you will need to consider if you have any transfer balance account reporting obligations when winding up your fund.

All SMSFs must report events that affect their member's transfer balance account. Your member's account is debited when they fully or partially commute a retirement phase income stream. This can be paid out of the super system in a lump sum, or it can be transferred to another fund. The value of this commutation needs to be reported to us on a super transfer balance account report (TBAR) at the time it occurs. When transferring retirement balances to another super fund, the transfer balance cap still applies. This applies to all super funds, whether SMSFs or APRA-regulated funds.

When winding up your SMSF, you need to have an audit completed by an approved SMSF auditor before you can lodge your final SMSF annual return. You need to lodge your SMSF annual return and complete Question 9 **Was the fund wound up during the income year?** in Section A.

You should also complete question M **Supervisory levy adjustment for wound up funds** in Section D. This reduces the SMSF supervisory levy that you must pay so that you do not pay the levy for the following year. You must also pay any outstanding tax liabilities and lodge any outstanding returns.

If you don't wind up your fund correctly you may be selected for compliance activities and subject to penalties. Where your member is rolling over their income stream to another fund, it is strongly encouraged for you to report this commutation to the ATO as early as possible. For example, if an SMSF member rolls their super benefit into an APRA-regulated fund and starts an income stream there – and it is not reported to the ATO by the SMSF at the time it happens – a double-counting of the member's income streams will occur. This is because there will be a mismatch in timing of the reporting done by the APRA-regulated fund and the SMSF. In this instance, an SMSF is encouraged to report the commutation as it occurs, or no later than at the time of the rollover.

To confirm that you have met all of your reporting and tax responsibilities, the ATO will send you a letter stating that it has:

- cancelled your SMSF's ABN
- closed your SMSF's record on the ATO systems.

You should not close your bank accounts until all expected final liabilities have been settled and requested refunds are received. Tax liabilities (including the supervisory levy) can be paid when you lodge the final SMSF annual return. After all amounts are certain and have been paid, then you can close your bank accounts.

References:

ATO Website:

https://www.ato.gov.au/super/self-managed-super-funds/winding-up/

https://www.ato.gov.au/Super/Self-managed-super-funds/Winding-up/Deal-with-members--benefits/

https://www.ato.gov.au/Super/Self-managed-super-funds/Winding-up/Arrange-a-final-audit-and-complete-your-reporting/

Concluding Remarks

I am sure that you still have a lot of questions after reading this insightful, educational book on SMSFs. It is good to write down the list of questions to take to your accountant or financial adviser at your next visit, or when you are ready, or want to clarify some things in relation to having an SMSF.

Perhaps you want your accountant or financial adviser to help you assess or determine whether this is the right way for you to go at this stage. They will give you a number of options, mention to you the advantages and disadvantages, but please note, it is your ultimate decision whether you wish to start a SMSF or not. This book is a helpful guide providing the ins and outs of having and maintaining a SMSF, but this book is only educational and a starting point to your many questions that you wish to raise with your professional accountant or adviser.

On another note, it should be clear that there is no law stating that you must have a minimum amount in order to start a SMSF, so when you hear your peers or associates mentioning that you need a minimum of at least $100,000 to $200,000, this is a myth. Obviously, this minimum is only a recommendation if you want your SMSF to be effective and provide you with the growth better than industry superfunds. Also, it depends on what you wish to do with a small amount of funds. A small amount will not allow you to borrow for investing in a property, but you can perhaps invest in shares, bonds, units in a unit trust (provided it is an investment unit trust), and other assets where small investments can be made.

Please note also that having a small balance may be taken up each year when you engage your accountant to prepare the accounts and annual return, and an independent auditor to sign off the financial accounts. These are all costly and if you do not make regular contributions, you will not benefit from your SMSF. You need to have clear goals and objectives before even commencing a SMSF and this needs to be clearly set up in the investment strategy. If the SMSF is not the way for you right now, it is not the end of the world, there may be a future opportunity to start a SMSF.

Appendix 1 - Case Example 1

SINGLE MEMBER SMSF

John is single, 40 years old and would like to commence a SMSF. He has super amounts across other funds totalling $40,000. His annual income from employment is $60,000 and his employer contributes 9.5% super guarantee of $5,700 into his fund. What are the options available for John in setting up a SMSF?

- He needs to determine the advantages and disadvantages of having a SMSF of this kind of amount, and the first thing he needs to ask is what is the objective of moving to a SMSF.
- Since he is single and will likely be the only member to benefit from the SMSF, according to the super law and regulations, he must set up a Company Trustee where he will be the sole director and shareholder of that company. The company will solely act as a trustee of the SMSF.
- If he wants to set up the SMSF as an individual trustee, then he must have another person, and that person must not be disqualified from being a trustee. The other person does not need to be a member of the SMSF.
- However, for more protection, the general recommendation is to set up a Company Trustee.
- After setting up the SMSF and opening a bank account, he needs to arrange for a rollover of benefits from his other fund/s into his SMSF and provide to the fund/s his SMSF details. The rollover benefit statement will show the different

components of his balance, i.e. tax-free and taxable component. He must keep this as a record.

- He then needs to inform his employer that his super details have changed and provide the employer with the new details, namely his SMSF bank account details, for his employer to pay the super into his SMSF. The employer contributions into his SMSF are taxed at 15%.

What are John's investment options?

Firstly, he must prepare an investment strategy stating the overall objective of the fund, mention the risks of such investments and how the risk/s can be overcome. He needs to also include an allocation range of types of investments he is considering. He needs to state the consideration of insurance premiums and mention why insurance is or is not appropriate.

After preparing the strategy, he then needs to implement this in his investments. For example, if his strategy states that he will have between 20% and 40% in cash and fixed interest, then he must ensure this type of investment falls within that range in proportion to his total super balance.

He may also decide to have 10% to 20% in listed shares, whether Australian or overseas. Again, he must ensure that the SMSF has that range of percentage in proportion to the overall super balance. He must consider that he can lose some or all of his capital if he has investments in listed shares. The only instance he can invest in unlisted shares is that it is a public company.

He may also like to consider investing in mortgage loans that provide a higher interest rate than traditional term deposits and savings accounts, but must consider that it is likely that he will lose some or all of his capital.

He can invest in a fixed unit trust that has property investment, and in turn the unit trust will distribute to his SMSF a portion of its profit each year, e.g. if his SMSF invests 20% in the unit trust, the trust will have to distribute 20% of its profits to the SMSF. The unit trust cannot be seen as operating a business, because this will breach the SIS regulations.

The other option John has is purchase a storage unit (commercial property) but he needs to consider factors such as rental returns, outgoings, tenancy lease terms, and whether it will benefit his SMSF in the long-term. This must also be included in his investment strategy.

Suppose he invests in shares and purchases a storage unit. Income derived from these investments is taxed at 15% because of his age and also his SMSF is in accumulation phase. Brokerage costs on shares are tax deductible. The outgoings that the SMSF will likely pay on the storage unit are tax deductible. If his SMSF generates an overall 10% - 12% return, then the SMSF has done quite well. If his SMSF generates about 5% to 7%, then he needs to do a bit of work in order to maximise the benefits that his SMSF has potential to generate.

Let us say that John's SMSF has $20,000 in shares and derives $2,000 in fully franked dividends. The franking credits attached total $857.14, assuming the companies that distributed the dividends pay 30% tax.

Also, the income from a storage unit investment that his SMSF purchased for $20,000 provided a NET return (after outgoings have been paid) of $1,300. The SMSF also has $8,000 in cash after paying expenses and obligations, namely the accounting and audit fees. His employer contributed $5,700 (9.5% of his gross wages of $60,000). The SMSF then paid $1,000 in accounting and audit fees. The net income of the fund is $2,000 + $857.14 + $1,300 + $5,700 - $1,000 = $8,857.00 (no need to include the cents). This amount is added as a profit allocation to his member statement.

First of all, how did we arrive at the cash balance? After John's SMSF invested the $40,000 in shares and storage unit, these investments provided the SMSF with $2,000 dividends, $1,300 net rent and $5,700 employer contributions, and the SMSF paid $1,000 accounting and audit fees, which makes the bank balance $8,000.

Market value of shares have increased to $25,000 and the storage unit increased to $21,000, so his super balance is $54,000 including the bank balance of $8,000. The $8,000 in the bank represents the net income of the fund, but we need to then add the franking credit of $857.14 to arrive at the member's super balance before tax of $54,857.14.

Now that we established the taxable income is $8,857, tax on this is 15%, which is $1,328.55. We then use the franking credits to reduce the tax liability, so subtract $857,14, which gives a total of 471.41. Because this is the first year that the SMSF will lodge a tax return to the ATO, the Supervisory Levy will be $518 ($259x2), so the total tax liability of the fund in the first year is $989.41. We then take a deferred tax based on the increase in market value ($6,000 x 15%) which is $900. His super balance after tax and after allowing for the $900 deferred tax is $52,967.59. He commenced with a balance of $40,000, so in the first year, after tax his SMSF grew by $12,967.59. If we take out the employer contribution of $5,700, the effective growth is $7,267.59. This is a very good growth in the first year of the SMSF.

Suppose in the following year, the SMSF has a beginning balance of $52,967.59 and John had a pay rise to $65,000 gross, but he wants to make a $5,000 salary sacrifice into his SMSF. Therefore his gross wages is back to $60,000, his tax will be the same as prior year, but his SMSF will have $5,000 in addition to the employer contribution of $5,700 (9.5% of $60,000), so his contribution to the SMSF will be $10,700 and this will be taxed at 15%. Let us say that he also chose to make an additional concessional contribution of $10,000. This means that his personal taxable income will now be $50,000 (or less if he applies other deductions in his tax return). The extra $10,000 contribution can be claimed as a deduction, and then his SMSF will pay 15% tax on this. Therefore, the total super contributions will be $20,700 and will be taxed at 15%. The components of this is employer contribution of $5,700, salary sacrifice contribution of $5,000 and additional personal concessional contributions of $10,000.

The SMSF paid the tax of $989.41 during the second year, so the bank balance before contributions is now $7,010.59. Total contributions for year 2 as per the above paragraph amount to $20,700, so hypothetically, the bank balance is $27,710.59.

John's SMSF sold some shares that he held for more than 12 months, and proceeds from sale amounted to $17,000. The purchase price of the shares was $10,000. The capital gain is $7,000, but since the SMSF held the shares for more than 12 months, tax on the capital gain is $700 (10%). The SMSF then invested $25,000 in a mortgage loan with an interest rate of 8% per annum paid monthly. The investment was made 3 months before the end of year 2, so his SMSF was paid 3 months interest, which means the amount is $500.00.

Dividends from the remaining shares amounted to $1,000 plus franking credits of $428.57. Let us now track his SMSF bank account. We began with $27,710.59 after accounting for all contributions, his SMSF sold shares for $17,000 but invested $25,000 in a mortgage loan. The bank balance is now $19,710.59. Let us say that he purchased another storage unit for $17,000. The bank balance is now $2,710.59.

During year 2, the following income was derived, minus the contributions:

- Dividends from shares $1,000 with franking credits $428.57
- Net rent from two storage units $1,700
- Interest from investment in mortgage loan $500
- Paid accounting and audit fees, and settlement costs of storage unit $1,900

Net bank statement activity is $1,300, suppose this is also the net income. Bank balance at end of year 2 is $2,710.59 plus $1,300 = $4,010.59.

The net income of the fund is $1,300 + $428.57 franking credits + $20,700 contributions + $7,000 capital gain = $29,428.57. Tax on the capital gain is $700, so the remaining amount that is subject to

15% tax is $22,428.57 = $3,364.29. Then we add $700 capital gains tax means the tax liability is $4,064.29, subtract the franking credits of $428.57 = $3,635.72 plus $259 ATO Supervisory Levy = $3,894.72 is the overall tax liability of the fund in year 2.

The remaining shares in the SMSF reduced to a market value of $9,000, which had a purchase price of $10,000. The storage unit that cost $20,000 in year 1 is now $22,000, and the other storage unit purchased for $17,000 is the same because it was purchased only four months before the end of year 2. Therefore, market value of the investments is $9,000 shares + $22,000 storage unit 1 + $17,000 storage unit 2 + $25,000 mortgage loan investment = $73,000. The market value of the shares remaining at the end of year 1 was $12,500, and now it is $9,000, so it reduced by $3,500. The storage unit increased by another $1,000, so the change in market value is $2,500 decrease. The tax effect on this is $375 deferred tax asset. In year 1 we had a deferred tax liability of $900, then $700 was taxed on the current capital gain, so the deferred tax is now $200 less $375 = $175 deferred tax asset.

Now we have the fund's assets as: $73,000 + the bank account $4,010.59 = $77,010.59. The SMSF also has a deferred tax asset of $175, so the total assets is $77,185.59. Income tax liability is $3,894.72, so the fund's net assets is $73,290.87. This figure should be the member's balance in John's member statement at the end of year 2.

The deferred tax figure may be confusing and may not be 100% accurate, but this is to the best of my knowledge. Regardless, it must still be present in every year where the SMSF has movements in investments that are subject to market movements, e.g. shares, property.

Now the SMSF has grown from $52,967.59 to $73,290.87 after John used salary sacrifice and personal concessional contribution provisions in year 2. This represents a growth of $12,625.85, in terms of percentage, it is a growth of 23.84%. The majority of this growth can be contributed to the fact that John had $20,700

contributions into his SMSF, in comparison with last year, only
$5,700 contributions.

Appendix 2 - Case Example 2

TWO MEMBERS IN ACCUMULATION PHASE

Jack and Jill are husband and wife, both in their mid 50s, and they
decide to set up a SMSF with both of them as members with a
Corporate Trustee. They are both in accumulation phase. In this

instance, both Jack and Jill must both be directors of the trustee Company. They both run a business out of a commercial property that is jointly owned by the two of them. Their business entity pays rent each month to them as they are both the landlords.

Jack and Jill decided that they would make the most use out of their SMSF by transferring the commercial property from their individual names into the SMSF. They also have a combined super balance of $100,000 in APRA regulated superfunds and they arranged for a rollover of benefits after opening up a bank account in the name of their SMSF.

As they both operate a business, having set up their SMSF, they contribute $50,000 ($25,000 each member) concessional contributions, which is taxed at 15%. As a result, their super balance is now $150,000. If their business is a company, the company will save 27.5% tax on the $50,000 super contribution and the SMSF pays 15% tax.

They transfer the commercial property from their names into the SMSF, as this is allowed under the super law for a member/s to transfer business real property into their SMSF. This is called an in-specie contribution. Jack and Jill will need to declare capital gains in their individual tax returns and the transfer is a deemed sale at market value. The SMSF then has to pay stamp duty on transfer at the market value of the property. No GST will be applicable on the price of the property because it is a going-concern, i.e. there are tenants occupying the property and operating a business.

Let us say that the property has a market value on $1,000,000. Rent return at market rates is 9%, so the rent for the year will be $90,000, which means the SMSF will have to register for GST and lodge quarterly Business Activity Statements (BAS). The $90,000 rent can be either inclusive of GST, or the SMSF will need to charge 10% on top of the $90,000, so the SMSF will have to remit $9,000 in GST to the tax office for the year via BAS lodgements.

In order to achieve the maximum benefit, Jack and Jill have a commercial agreement between their SMSF and their business in which the business will pay the rent plus the outgoings of the premises, so the SMSF will not have to bear the expenses, i.e. insurance, rates, land tax, etc. This is allowable provided the agreement is clear and sets out the duty and responsibility of both tenant and landlord.

Jack and Jill also created an SMSF share trading account with their bank and invested in a share and managed funds portfolio for $100,000 and have diversified their allocations very well. Their shares proportion is about 10% of the fund's total assets, and shares are liquid assets that can easily be converted into cash. The shares and managed funds derived income of $10,000 comprising of dividends, other income and foreign income, of which franking credits and foreign tax credits total $3,448.00.

By the end of the financial year, the SMSF has the following income:

- Rent $90,000 (NET of GST)
- Concessional contributions $50,000
- Income from shares and managed funds $10,000 (plus franking and foreign tax credits of $3,448)
- Expenses - accounting and audit fees $2,000

Net profit of the fund is $148,000 which will be taxed at 15% = $22,200.

If this was a net profit of the company, the company tax at 27.5% would have been $40,700.

If this was a net profit/taxable income in the names of the individuals, they will pay marginal rates of tax, which is higher than the SMSF and company tax. You can now see the strategy in tax saving when the assets that generate income are in the name of the SMSF.

Let us go back to the SMSF tax of $22,200. The franking and foreign tax credits of $3,448 are subtracted, which gives a total of $18,752.00. We need to add the ATO Supervisory Levy of $518

($259 x 2 because this is the first year of the fund), which means the overall tax payable of the fund is $19,270.

If we look at the income generated by the property, $90,000 rent and the market value is $1 million, the return is 9%. The income from shares and managed fund investments of $10,000 with the purchase price of $100,000 is a 10% return. When we average the two percentages, the average return for the fund is 9.5%, which is not bad at all.

The fund now has the following assets:

- Business real property market value $1,000,000 (no change)
- Shares and managed investments portfolio market value $95,000 (has decreased by $5,000)
- Bank account balance $40,000 (this figure is made up as an example)
- Deferred tax asset of $750 as a result of decrease in market value of $5,000

Total assets of the fund is $1,135,750.

The following liabilities of the fund:

- Income tax payable $19,270
- GST payable for final quarter of the financial year $2,250 (multiply by 4 quarters gives $9,000 total GST to be remitted to the ATO).

Total liabilities of the fund is $21,520.

The net assets of the fund is $1,114,230 which represents the members benefits in the SMSF.

Let us say that in the second year, Some of the investments of the shares are sold at a capital gain. As long as the shares are held for at least 12 months, the tax on the capital gain is 10%. Please refer to appendix 1 example on sale of shares.

Appendix 3 - Case Example 3

TWO MEMBERS IN PENSION PHASE

Following on from the previous case example of Jack and Jill, they are now both in their 60s and transfer some of their accumulation balance into an account-based pension. Let us say that Jack now has a pension balance of $400,000 and Jill has a pension balance of $500,000. The combined pension balance is $900,000. This leaves the accumulation balance at the beginning of year 2 of $214,230.

In chapter 5 (different phases of super) once a pension phase commences, this triggers what we call a transfer balance cap that was introduced with the effective date 1 July 2017 and the cap is $1,600,000 for each individual. Therefore, Jack and Jill have a cap of $1,600,000 each. Jack transfers $400,000 to his pension account, which means his cap is now $1,200,000. Jill transfers $500,000 to her pension account, meaning that her cap is now $1,100,000.

Suppose that the fund now generates $95,000 rent from the business real property (NET of GST) and derives income of $12,000 from shares and managed funds, with franking credits and foreign tax credits totalling $3,600. Some shares are sold at a capital gain of $10,000.

Jack and Jill both need to draw at least 2% (due to the COVID-19 which previously was 4%). They both met the minimum withdrawal rates and the pensions are tax-free. Jack took $35,000 and Jill took $45,000 tax-free pensions, and they both reduced their work hours significantly. They can still make concessional and non-concessional contributions.

Let us say now that the Jack's member balance at the beginning of the year is $500,000 and Jill's member balance at the beginning is $614,230. Jack's pension balance is $400,000 and Jill's pension balance is $500,000. The tax-free portions in the SMSF is as follows:

- Jack: $400,000/$500,000 * 100 = 80%
- Jill: $500,000/$614,230 * 100 = 81.40%

The average tax-free portion is around 80.70%. Let us say that the total income derived in the SMSF is as follows:

- Rent $95,000
- Shares & managed fund income $12,000 + $3,600 franking and foreign tax credits
- Capital gain $10,000 (tax-exempt portion is 80.70%, so the taxable portion of the capital gain is $1,930 taxed at 10%, which is $193.
- Combined concessional contributions $20,000

Total income of the fund $89,400 plus $20,000 contribution which is taxed at 15%.

In the SMSF tax return, we state that there is exempt pension income of $89,400 * 80.70% = $72,146. Subtract this from $89,400, giving a taxable income of $17,254 plus $20,000 concessional contribution = $37,254.00. The tax on the capital gain is $193, so the tax on remaining income will be 15% of $27,254, which is $4,088.10. Subtract the franking and foreign tax credits of $3,600, which means the tax payable is $488.10 + $193 capital gain tax + $259 ATO Supervisory Levy = $940.10 is the overall tax of the fund. There is still some tax because the fund has a combined accumulation and pension phase.

If the fund was in full pension phase (100% pension), there will be no concessional contributions, and therefore the exempt pension income will be 100% of the income derived in the SMSF. The only tax that the SMSF will pay is $259 Supervisory Levy, and the rest of the franking and foreign tax credits are refundable to the SMSF. This provision is not available in a normal trust structure, where there is 100% exempt income. It is only available in a superannuation fund.

Appendix 4 - Case Example 4

SINGLE MEMBER IN TRANSITION TO RETIREMENT PHASE

Jennifer is a single person aged 58, and has reached her preservation age according to the ATO's preservation table. She is still employed but on a part-time basis as she is reducing her work hours. She already has her own SMSF with a company trustee structure and has $600,000 as her member balance in the SMSF at 1 July 2019.

She decided to commence a transition to retirement phase account, which does not trigger a transfer balance cap.

What are her withdrawal options during the 2019-20 financial year so that she does not pay tax?

One of the options is to withdraw a lump sum amount of up to $210,000 without paying tax. This figure is the low rate cap available for a person who commences a transition to retirement. Chapter 5 discusses in more detail the tax on benefits received while in transition to retirement.

The earnings in the SMSF are still taxed at 15%, and there is no exempt pension income because Jennifer is not yet at retirement age.

What if she wants to take an income stream, i.e. take an amount each month, with total withdrawal $80,000?

We need to determine what the tax-free component of her balance is. Let us say that the tax-free component of her $600,000 balance is $250,000 and her taxable component is $350,000. The tax-free percentage of her balance is 41.67% and the taxable component is 58.33%. We must use these percentages to reflect the proper taxable component of her withdrawal. We cannot state that $80,000 is all tax-free. The way it is calculated is: $80,000 * 41.67% = $33,336 is the tax-free amount, so she will be taxed on $46,664.00.

What is the tax rate on the taxable amount of $46,664? The tax rate is her marginal rate, plus Medicare Levy, less a 15% tax offset. Suppose her marginal tax rate is 32.5%, add Medicare Levy, this means she will pay 34.5% marginal tax rate on $46,664, which is $16,099. There is a 15% offset available on $46,664, which amounts to $6,999.60. After subtracting the offset from the tax payable, the overall tax on this super withdrawal is $9,099.40. We can see that she will be disadvantaged if she chooses to take an income stream. She could take $80,000 as a lump sum and this will all be tax-free, provided that she does not withdraw multiple times during the year.

Of-course, if she was at retirement age and the SMSF is in pension phase, any amount she withdraws will be tax-free, whether it is a lump-sum or whether it is income stream, but she has to comply with the minimum withdrawal requirements.

What if Jennifer wanted to withdraw a lump sum of $240,000? The first $210,000 will be tax-free, but she will be taxed on the $30,000 excess, based on her marginal rate plus Medicare Levy, or 17% tax, whichever is lower. From the example, her marginal rate is 34.5%. However, since 17% is the lower rate, we use this and arrive at a tax amount of $5,100.00. There is no offset available on the excess lump sum withdrawal.

In concluding this example, Jennifer's best option is to take a lump sum up to the low rate cap of $210,000, which will all be tax-free.

www.ingramcontent.com/pod-product-compliance
Lightning Source LLC
Chambersburg PA
CBHW071029220526
45467CB00004B/1577